Family Ties

By the Editors of Time-Life Books

Alexandria, Virginia

TIME®
LIFE
BOOKS

Time-Life Books Inc.
is a wholly owned subsidiary of

Time Incorporated

FOUNDER: Henry R. Luce 1898-1967

Editor-in-Chief: Henry Anatole Grunwald
Chairman and Chief Executive Officer:
J. Richard Munro
President and Chief Operating Officer:
N. J. Nicholas, Jr.
Chairman of the Executive Committee:
Ralph P. Davidson
Corporate Editor: Ray Cave
Executive Vice President, Books: Kelso F. Sutton
Vice President, Books: George Artandi

Time-Life Books Inc.

EDITOR: George Constable
Executive Editor: Ellen Phillips
Director of Design: Louis Klein
Director of Editorial Resources: Phyllis K. Wise
Editorial Board: Russell B. Adams, Jr., Dale M.
Brown, Roberta Conlan, Thomas H. Flaherty, Lee
Hassig, Donia Ann Steele, Rosalind Stubenberg, Kit
van Tulleken, Henry Woodhead
Director of Photography and Research:
John Conrad Weiser

PRESIDENT: Christopher T. Linen
Chief Operating Officer: John M. Fahey, Jr.
Senior Vice President: James L. Mercer
Vice Presidents: Stephen L. Bair, Ralph J. Cuomo,
Neal Goff, Stephen L. Goldstein, Juanita T. James,
Hallett Johnson III, Carol Kaplan, Susan J.
Maruyama, Robert H. Smith, Paul R. Stewart,
Joseph J. Ward
Director of Production Services:
Robert J. Passantino

Library of Congress Cataloging in Publication Data
Family Ties.
  (Successful parenting)
  Bibliography: p.
  Includes index.
  1. Family—United States. 2. Parenting—United
States.
I. Time-Life Books. II. Series.
HQ536.F3785 1987 306.8'5'0973 87-19081
ISBN 0-8094-5941-8
ISBN 0-8094-5942-6 (lib. bdg.)

Successful Parenting

SERIES DIRECTOR: Dale M. Brown
Series Administrator: Norma E. Shaw
Editorial Staff for *Family Ties*
Designer: Raymond Ripper
Picture Editor: Blaine Marshall
Text Editors: Robert A. Doyle and John Newton
Staff Writer: Margery A. duMond
Researchers: Charlotte Fullerton (principal), Fran
Moshos, Nancy C. Scott
Assistant Designer: Susan M. Gibas
Copy Coordinator: Ruth Baja Williams
Picture Coordinator: Linda Yates
Editorial Assistants: Jenester C. Lewis and Pat
Whiteford

Special Contributors: Amy Aldrich, Ronald H.
Bailey, Lois Gilman, Donal Kevin Gordon, Wendy
Murphy, Susan Perry, Marian Smith Holmes (text);
Susan Blair, Barbara Cohn, Elizabeth Kupersmith,
Anne Muñoz-Furlong (research)

Editorial Operations
Copy Chief: Diane Ullius
Production: Celia Beattie
Library: Louise D. Forstall

Correspondents: Elisabeth Kraemer-Singh (Bonn);
Maria Vincenza Aloisi (Paris); Ann Natanson
(Rome)

First printing. Printed in U.S.A.

Published simultaneously in Canada.
School and library distribution by
Silver Burdett Company, Morristown,
New Jersey 07960.

TIME-LIFE is a trademark of Time
Incorporated U.S.A.

Other Publications:

TIME FRAME
FIX IT YOURSELF
FITNESS, HEALTH & NUTRITION
HEALTHY HOME COOKING
UNDERSTANDING COMPUTERS
LIBRARY OF NATIONS
THE ENCHANTED WORLD
THE KODAK LIBRARY OF CREATIVE PHOTOGRAPHY
GREAT MEALS IN MINUTES
THE CIVIL WAR
PLANET EARTH
COLLECTOR'S LIBRARY OF THE CIVIL WAR
THE EPIC OF FLIGHT
THE GOOD COOK
WORLD WAR II
HOME REPAIR AND IMPROVEMENT
THE OLD WEST

*For information on and a full description of any
of the Time-Life Books series listed above, please
call 1-800-621-7026, or write:*
Reader Information
Time-Life Customer Service
P.O. Box C-32068
Richmond, Virginia 23261-2068

This volume is one of a series about raising children.

The Consultants

Dr. Constance R. Ahrons advised on the section dealing with alternative family patterns *(pages 100–117)*. She is associate professor and associate director of the Marriage and Family Therapy Program at the University of Southern California at Los Angeles. A practicing family therapist in Santa Monica, she has focused in her research and writing on the question of how families restructure themselves after divorce. She is coauthor of *Divorced Families: A Multidisciplinary Developmental View.*

Dr. Kathleen Alison Clarke-Stewart assisted with the chart detailing the child's social-emotional development within the family *(pages 28–37)*. She is professor and associate director of the Program in Social Ecology at the University of California, Irvine. Dr. Clarke-Stewart is affiliated with the Society for Research in Child Development and with the American Psychological Association. A frequent contributor to professional journals, she also wrote *Daycare,* which is available in three languages, and *Child Development: Infancy through Adolescence.*

Dr. Judith Frances Dunn, Professor of Human Development at the Pennsylvania State University, helped develop the section on sibling bonds *(pages 54–83)*. A former Fellow of King's College, University of Cambridge, Dr. Dunn was one of the first scientists to conduct a major longitudinal study of siblings. She is a consulting editor for *Developmental Psychology* and for *Child Development.* Among her writings on sibling relationships are the books, *Sisters and Brothers* and *Siblings: Love, Envy, and Understanding,* coauthored with Carol Kendrick.

Dr. Sherman Elias, a physician specializing in genetics, obstetrics, and gynecology, gave his expert advice on sex selection *(box, page 49)*. Dr. Elias is the director of the Division of Reproductive Genetics, as well as professor and associate chairman for Academic Affairs and Research, at the University of Tennessee College of Medicine. His published works include *Reproductive Genetics and the Law,* written with Professor George Annas of the Boston University School of Medicine.

Dr. Michael E. Lamb, an internationally known expert on child and family development, assisted with the sections on the functions and growth of a family *(pages 6–19 and 38–49)*, and also with the essay on spacing children *(pages 50–53)*. He is chief of the Section on Social and Emotional Development in the National Institute of Child Health and Human Development, Bethesda, Maryland. A member of the editorial boards of *Infant Behavior and Development* and *Developmental Psychology,* Dr. Lamb is author or coauthor of more than 300 research articles and professional papers, and editor or coeditor of twenty-four books. Among his works are *The Father's Role: Applied Perspectives* and *The Father's Role: Cross-Cultural Perspectives.*

Dr. Hamilton McCubbin helped prepare the section on handling family stress *(pages 84–99)*. He is professor and dean of the School of Family Resources and Consumer Sciences at the University of Wisconsin at Madison and director of the university's Family Stress, Coping and Health Project. Dr. McCubbin, who has conducted extensive research on the functioning of families under stress, is president of the National Council on Family Relations and is an associate editor of *The Journal of Marriage and Family.* His published works include *Marriage and the Family: Individuals and Life Cycles,* written with Barbara Dahl.

Dr. Ross D. Parke, professor of Psychology at the University of Illinois at Urbana-Champaign, provided his view on fathering *(box, page 17)*. Dr. Parke is the editor of *Developmental Psychology* and has served on the editorial boards of several other scholarly journals. He has conducted original research on the interactions of infants and their fathers. His book *Fathers,* first published in 1981, has since been translated into six languages.

Dr. Robert Plomin, who contributed to the essay on genetics *(pages 20-27)*, is professor of Human Development at the Pennsylvania State University. A past secretary of the Behavior Genetics Association, Dr. Plomin has written extensively on the inheritability of temperament, personality, and intelligence, as well as physical traits. He is the author of *Development, Genetics, and Psychology.*

Dr. Rudolph Schaffer, an internationally recognized authority on parent-child interaction and infant behavior and socialization, provided his view on mothering *(box, page 16)*. Professor of Psychology at the University of Strathclyde in Glasgow, Scotland, Dr. Schaffer is a Fellow of the British Psychological Society and serves on the editorial boards of *Developmental Psychology* and the *Journal of Child Psychology and Psychiatry.* His published works include his books *Mothering* and *The Child's Entry into a Social World.*

Dr. Nick Stinnett, consultant for the section on family unity *(pages 118-139)*, is professor of Human Development and Family Life at the College of Human Environmental Sciences at the University of Alabama in Tuscaloosa. He is also the founder of the Center for Building Family Strengths at the University of Nebraska in Lincoln. A frequent speaker on family life, Dr. Stinnett in 1986 received the Mace Medal Award for outstanding service to families. His published works include *Secrets of Strong Families,* written with John DeFrain.

Gregory D. Sullivan, a certified public accountant and certified financial planner, is the president and chief executive officer of Derand Wealth Advisors, a financial planning firm in Arlington, Virginia. He helped develop the material on the financial aspects of family planning *(pages 44-45)*. A member of the International Association for Financial Planning and of the Registry of Financial Planning Practitioners, Mr. Sullivan makes frequent radio and television appearances to discuss family financial matters. His advice has been featured in *Money* magazine.

Contents

Laying the Foundations

With the arrival of your first child, you and your partner no longer are just a couple, as the pair at right has happily discovered, but members of a new family with a life and future all your own. For your youngster, the family will play fully as important a role in his development as the genes he inherited through you and your spouse. It will, at the very least, constitute his external world for many years to come and provide the environment in which he will begin to explore his own identity and develop his own humanity.

Of what should the world of your family consist? And how can you provide for your little explorer's needs, encourage the development of his personality and talents, yet still answer your own sometimes conflicting needs as wife/mother or husband/father?

Answers to these and many other questions concerning family life are offered in the text that follows. You will learn how genetic inheritance, environmental influences, and the forces of physical and emotional development combine to shape personality, and how the family evolves as the child— and parents—mature together. And most reassuring of all, you will discover that, despite many changes in the family unit over recent decades, the basic structure remains sturdy. Why? Because children's needs for love, security, self-discipline, socialization, and self-worth remain the same, and those are the very gifts that a family has always been best equipped to offer.

The Nature of Families

Families fulfill a basic human need. "Just as deer and buffalo are herding animals, fish are schooling animals, and birds are flocking animals, human beings," says anthropologist Paul Bohannan, "are family animals. It's in our fibre, one of the behavioral dimensions of our genes." Indeed, as far back in time as human knowledge reaches, people have lived in families. Empires have risen and fallen, religions waxed and waned, economic systems come and gone. Yet the family has always remained—small wonder Margaret Mead called it history's "toughest institution."

From its origins in the ancient past, the family continues to fulfill one fundamental purpose—to perpetuate the species by establishing an environment in which adults can not only create the next generation, but also nurture and socialize the young until they are able to manage successfully on their own.

Differing structures In a changing world, the family itself is changing. In the most traditional setup, the nucleus remains a mother and a father who share the same dwelling along with one or more children whom they rear together. The mother stays home while the father goes out to work; often his job is near enough to make him an important presence in the household. Ranged around this nucleus are members of the extended family—grandparents, aunts, uncles, and cousins.

While the traditional family survives, it is growing smaller, with fewer children being born. At the same time, more and more mothers are working outside the home. Often jobs for both spouses involve a long commute, which cuts down on the time each can spend with the children. The day-to-day interplay among relatives that once was usual has given way to long-distance telephone calls, letters, and holiday visits, as circumstances scatter loved ones across the map.

In the meantime, new family configurations are becoming increasingly prevalent. Single-parent families are on the rise; so are families in which a caregiver takes over part of the working mother's domestic role. There are also communal families, such as the kibbutzim of Israel, where the parents have a special responsibility for their children but delegate the primary child rearing to professionals.

One for all— all for one Though changing, the family still provides the framework by which each member can be recognized as an individual and yet be part of an interdependent group where unconditional love is assured. Providing for the individual needs of separateness and connectedness is never easy, and in a healthy family it is never finished. The two conditions are by nature contradictory; in order for each family member to get what he requires, others must at times make sacrifices or, at the least, curb selfish desires. When parents have small children, for example, they must give up some of their own individual needs in order to provide for their youngsters' physical and emotional well-being. But in doing so, they experience a sense of completeness, a feeling of purpose that provides life with new meaning.

The family in society Parents have always been the most important agents of socialization of their children. Parental influence occurs not in a vacuum, however, but within the framework of the larger society, with which the parents identify. By following their parents' example and learning how to conform to society's standards, children gain a strong sense of identity. This influence, together with the security they gain from being well loved, is one of the most compelling justifications for the existence of the family. ❖

Changing Trends in Family Structure

The family is a dynamic institution, constantly adapting to new social and economic conditions. In recent decades, the American family has been dramatically reshaped by three powerful trends (chart at right).

As the number of children born declines sharply, family size shrinks (red line), with two offspring now average for a couple. At the same time, more and more youngsters have mothers who work outside the home (blue line). And more children than ever before live with just one parent (green line) as separations, divorces, and out-of-wedlock births continue to increase.

Through other changes not tracked here, more children today live in blended families, with stepparents and stepsiblings; more first children are born to mothers over thirty; and more nuclear families reside in places distant from grandparents and other kin.

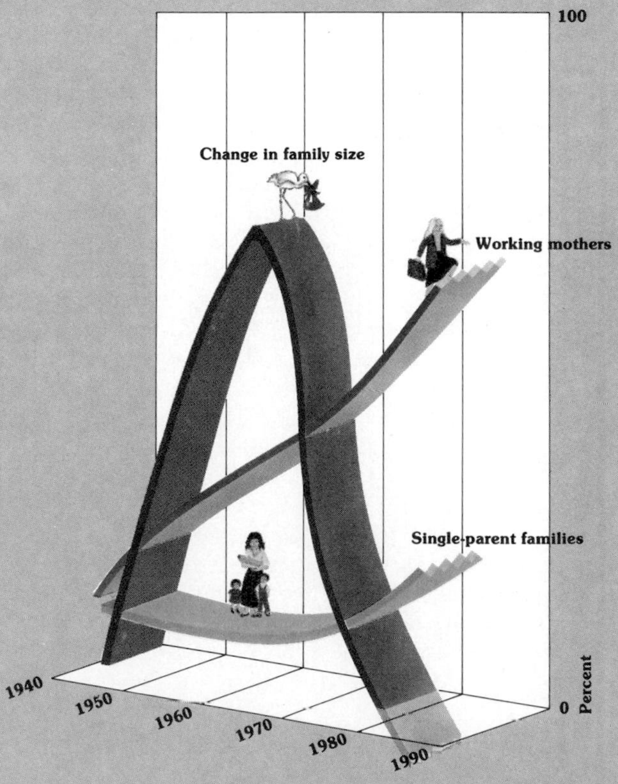

Change in family size

Working mothers

Single-parent families

100

Percent

0

1940 1950 1960 1970 1980 1990

The Family in Action

No other animal species has a longer period of dependency and youth than homo sapiens. Birds fly days after hatching; foals stand up and run about within minutes of being born. But the human baby is helpless much of her first year, and almost two decades must pass before a child can be said to be ready to leave the family fold.

During the early phase of this period, he is particularly susceptible to his parents' influence. In this network of inter-dependent relationships, they provide much of what he needs for future survival. Sheltered by their love, warmth, and nurturing, he gradually absorbs their attitudes, values, and beliefs. Responding to their praise and criticism, he learns how to express his emotions, how to behave, how to react to others. Within the closed circle of the family, he discovers who he is, developing a self-image, a sexual identity, and a sense of self-esteem. He also finds out what he is, as reflected by his social class, religion, and race. And if his parents are supportive of it, he begins to realize his intellectual potential. In a word, the child becomes civilized.

This process of becoming, or as the scientists call it, socialization, is a dynamic one. It ensures that the members of one generation will shape the personalities and behaviors of the next and that society will be preserved. Thanks to the family, a child acquires most of what he needs to know to survive as an adult, including the skills to get along outside the family.

The family by its dynamic nature is always in a state of flux, continually challenged by internal events. Change is constant, stimulated by innumerable variables. For one thing, parents, separately and together, continually bring their different expectations and personalities to bear on their offspring. The children in turn have a deep effect on their parents. The arrival of each new child produces further change, modifying the family mix through the impact of her temperament, sex, and eventually the relationship she has with her siblings.

Parents as molders of children and vice versa

In rearing children, parents are likely to resort to one of three common parenting styles—the authoritarian, the permissive, or the authoritative—and these can produce very different results. Authoritarian parents are parent-centered and demanding. They require their child to follow their orders without question and discourage verbal give-and-take when conflicts arise; they basically believe that allowing the child to "win" on any point is an indication of weakness. They are often reluctant to show affection or to praise, and they may tend to use physical punishment as the primary means of enforcing discipline.

Permissive parents, by contrast, are child-centered. They make few demands on their youngster, avoid conflicts whenever possible, view the child's impulses as natural and unavoidable, and generally tailor their lives to the tempo the child sets.

Authoritative parents are also child-centered but at the same time demanding. While they set high standards for responsible behavior, they are willing to discuss the reasons for their rules and regulations with their youngster. They display both warmth and consistent discipline, finding no contradiction in the two. The authoritative style has been shown to generate the greatest social competence in children.

Sometimes different parenting styles come into conflict, as in families where each parent has a different child-rearing orientation. When this happens, the youngster receives confusing and contradictory messages that put a strain on his loyalties and muddle his budding efforts to see order in the world. For that reason, parents with different approaches to child rearing should make every effort to agree about their goals and styles.

Even when parents follow generally similar parenting styles—and not all do—they are almost certain to bring different influences to bear on their children. This diversity is in itself beneficial, giving a youngster his first knowledge that adults are not all the same and that he, too, can be different.

The mere fact that mothers and fathers assume different roles in the family ensures that the treatment of the child will vary from the start. Mothers, for example, traditionally engage their little ones in a gentle form of face-to-face play, touching toes, fingers, and nose frequently, as though conducting some sort of inventory, or repeating words and phrases in soft tones. Fathers are far more likely to roughhouse, tossing their youngsters in the air, taking them on exaggerated rides, bouncing and poking and making loud silly noises. Baby responds differently to each parent, smiling contentedly at Mommy, greeting Daddy with wide eyes, giggles, and excited arm-waving.

These contrasting play styles may be biologically founded. Monkey fathers, for example, also engage in roughhousing, suggesting that this is ingrained male primate behavior. Mothers may just not be temperamentally or physically inclined toward such an active kind of play. Traditional fathers, in having less frequent intimate contact with their offspring, such as dressing, feeding, bathing, and carrying them around, may need to concentrate on more impressionable fun activities to engage and influence their youngsters. Some theorists believe

that fathers serve to draw the child away from his close attachment to his mother—and into the world. As every experienced mother or father knows, the relationship between parent and offspring has two sides to it: What the child does affects what the parent does and vice versa. You have only to think about how dramatically your own life changed when your first child arrived. Your infant's crying may have brought you running day and night. However young your baby may have been at the time, he taught you about his needs, showed you the ways in which you could soothe him, obliging you to modify your lifestyle and make all the sacrifices that were necessary for his comfort.

An authoritarian mother tells her son to put the bike away "because I said so." Authoritarian parents value unquestioning obedience; their children tend to be dependent and in reaction may become angry and defiant in later years.

The unique character traits of a child further influence a parent and affect the way he or she relates to the child. The mother who happily finds that her pride and joy reflects her temperament exactly is likely to have positive feelings toward him and show a natural ease in handling him. On the other hand, the parent and child may not be well matched. An active parent, for example, may have difficulty relating to an inactive, slow-to-warm-up youngster. A reserved parent may feel overwhelmed by an aggressive, excitable baby. A little insight can help smooth the transition period as the parent becomes accustomed to the child.

Additional influences on child and parent

The parent-child relationship can be affected still further by the makeup of the family itself. First children typically receive more attention from their mothers and fathers than their siblings, and they also tend to be disciplined more often. They may feel greater pressure placed on them for achievement, with their parents often holding them to a higher standard than their brothers and sisters. Spacing between births (*pages 50-53*), the sexes of the children, and the nature of the relationships among siblings, whether positive and supportive or dominated by rivalry and hostility, may additionally shape parents' attitudes toward their off-spring—and the children's attitudes toward their parents as well.

Repeating your past Sometimes hidden forces come into play. Every adult carries inside himself the imprint of his childhood relationships with his own parents and siblings. One psychologist has called this the "inner child."

If a young mother has happy memories of her childhood and feels good about the way in which she connected to her parents and siblings and they to her, for instance, she will understandably look for ways to recreate that happy experience within her own family. She may model her mothering upon her mother's example, look to her husband to be the kind of father that Daddy was, and expect her children to manifest the same comfortable and accepting relationship she had—or thinks she had—with her own parents and siblings. But within that set of expectations there lie potential pitfalls.

A different adult may come to parenthood burdened with an "inner child" whose feelings of anger or disappointment toward her own parents and siblings remain unresolved. A mother may swear that she will never repeat their mistakes, and then discover (or worse, be unaware) that she is visiting those very same sins on the next generation. Or she may go to opposite extremes and parent in a way that is artificial or notably different but curiously unsupportive of the child she ostensibly wants to guide and protect.

The examples of this kind of resolve gone awry are legion. Take the mother who still harbors feelings of resentment toward an older brother, perceived by her as the favored child when they were growing up. Now as an adult she may unwittingly take out that resentment on her son by being unduly harsh on him, but treat her daughter all too permissively. Or consider the father whose role model was a cold, authoritarian head of the household, who kept everyone at arm's length by being a stern critic and disciplinarian. The son may find it difficult to establish a warm, close connection to his own sons and daughters, having no example to draw upon, or he may make a conscious effort to reject the model and wind

An authoritative mother enlists her child's cooperation by providing a reason for her requests: "Please put your bike away so it won't get wet in the rain." Children who are raised by authoritative parents tend to be autonomous, friendly, and agreeable.

up instead so passive in his paternal role as to make his children feel unloved by him.

Getting rid of the inner child

To be wholly effective, parent-child relationships must draw their strength from the recognition that each member of the family has a personality and temperament all his own. Particularly in the beginning, when you are embarking on parenthood, your family's interests, as well as your own, will best be served if you keep expectations to a minimum.

If you were indeed fortunate enough to have had a mother and father whose manner of parenting you still admire, you cannot help bringing something of that style to your own children's upbringing. But try not to impose it too rigidly. Be tolerant enough to allow your partner and your children to settle naturally into their roles as best befits them.

If, however, you suspect yourself of harboring an inner child, of having a hidden or unconscious side to your parenting, make a deliberate effort to identify what issues might be involved. Ask yourself some hard questions: Do you lose your temper more frequently with one child than with another? Do you play favorites? Do you harbor jealous feelings when a grandparent showers your son or daughter with attention? Do you challenge your mate's authority in front of your youngster? And do you divide up parenting tasks so that your partner is always obliged to take on the bad-guy role? Are you constantly critical of your children, saying too often "That's nice, but," or so demanding of them that they never experience the gratification of pleasing you? Do any of these behaviors remind you of your own upbringing? If so, the time may have come for you to identify them for what they are and make a serious effort to modify them. For some parents, recognizing the source of a problem may be enough to motivate a behavioral change. For others, outside counseling may be needed to bring a problem to the

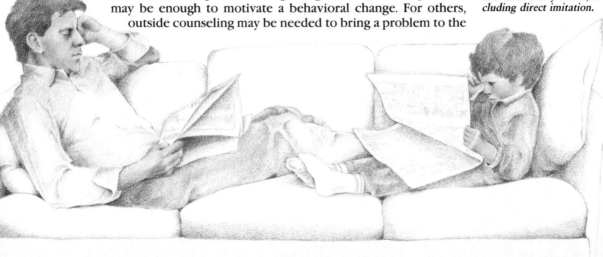

A little boy relaxing on the couch with the Sunday papers just like Daddy is practicing to be a man. Identification with the same-sex parent begins very early and takes many forms, including direct imitation.

Parents as gender models One of the greatest influences a parent can have on a child is in the area of sexual identification. Just as you learned from your father's or mother's example, so your child will learn from yours. He will also learn, of course, from those around him—his friends, teachers, and even people in movies and on television. But your example will be the greatest single determinant of his sexual identity. Thus the closer and warmer your relationship with the child, the larger your impact on him.

surface and resolve it.

A preschooler follows her mother's example and nurses her doll. Such identification springs from the loving relationship she has with her mother and will enhance her own mother role years hence.

For example, while a father may have a strong influence on his son, he can have an almost equally strong one on his daughter. Studies have shown that fathers who are very masculine tend to rear daughters who are highly feminine, the daughters learning how to complement their fathers' maleness with their own feminity.

Boys under five whose fathers have died or left the family are more likely to grow up less conventionally masculine than those whose fathers are a continuing influence in the home. When a boy deprived of a father has an uncle, a grandfather, or even a male neighbor to observe, he is in a better position to acquire a full male identity. (The absence of a father seems to have little effect on the gender development of a girl under five.)

Vying with one parent for the other's love Around the third birthday, boys and girls begin to seek answers to questions about their sexual identity. Beyond the infantile attachment children feel for their parents as caregivers and guarantors of their security, there may now be a strong sexual attraction to the parent of the opposite sex. A son may fantasize about taking his father's place as the object of his mother's affections or a daughter her mother's place. Some children verbalize a wish to marry the opposite-sex parent.

Such fantasies can create troubling tensions, often more pronounced in boys than in girls. The child may be torn by feelings of rivalry toward the parent of the same sex. While in the throes of this secret struggle a son, in particular, may defy or accuse his father and then feel guilty and ashamed.

During this phase, a parent should react calmly to the child's feelings. She should treat them as real but offer him the reassurance that his parents will always be his parents and that the love between marriage partners is different from the love of parent and child. Tell him that when he grows up it will be his turn to find someone to marry just as special as the parent to whom he feels so drawn.

In due course, usually between five and six, the child will abandon the romantic attachment to one parent and the conflict will resolve itself. Accepting that they can never take the place of their same-sex parent, children who go through this phase do the next best thing, which is: to become like Mom or Dad. The son may form a new attachment to his father based upon identification with the grownup's attitudes and behaviors; similarly, the daughter attaches herself more deeply to her mother than before.

An Expert's View

Redefining Motherhood

The concept of mother as saint long has been an icon of society. But now changes in the way we live and work call that image into question. What is mothering? What are mothers for? Does nature dictate that their role be based on gender and reproduction only, or is it one that can be extended and enhanced? At first sight, answers to such questions might seem obvious, for we are dealing with one of the universals of humankind—a relationship that occurs naturally, runs its course spontaneously, and of which everyone has some personal knowledge. We tend to take mothering for granted, explain it as instinctual, and shrug off instances of maternal neglect and cruelty as occasional aberrations that occur in any universal pattern.

Yet, on closer examination, there is nothing simple about mothering. Mother has variously been seen as teacher, benevolent spirit, guide, nurse, judge, dictator, democrat, provider of food, and protector against danger. To say she is all of these is both true and useless— true, because she indeed fulfills such functions; useless, because such a catalog gives but little indication of the remarkable nature of the mother-child interaction through which the baby begins to be assimilated into the world.

A mother's relationship with her child is that of a partner, albeit a senior partner, by virtue of her being more experienced and powerful. She is capable of acute awareness of her child's needs and can mold her own behavior very precisely to those needs. The younger the child, the greater is the need for the mother to adapt. It is one of the wonders of nature that mothers make the adjustments necessary so naturally and spontaneously that they themselves are often not fully aware they have made them. Whether we observe a mother feeding her baby, playing with him, bathing him, changing him, and putting him to bed, or merely bouncing him on her knee, we are struck by the fact that mother and child are engaged in a unique, highly intricate pattern of human interaction.

However wonderful and satisfying this may be for both, does it necessarily follow that mother must be her infant's constant companion throughout the day and night? Clearly some minimum period of togetherness is required, but there is nothing absolute about how much. Beyond the minimum, it is the personal qualities the mother brings to the interaction that count most.

Provided these qualities are given full play, there is no reason why mother and infant should not spend a portion of each day apart—the mother at work, the child at some form of day care or other arrangement with which the family is comfortable.

It may well be, of course, that such arrangements place a greater burden on the mother to get thoroughly acquainted with her baby during the limited time they spend together; it may also be that the fatigue brought on by working full-time outside the home will make it more difficult for her to respond sensitively to her child in the shortened time they are in each other's company at the beginning and end of the day. But such considerations must be weighed against the disadvantages of the mother's not going out to work or of the child's not being sent to day care. For the well-loved child, there are many arguments in favor of widening his interpersonal horizon and increasing his experience through contact with people outside the home and very few against good-quality day care.

Rudolph Schaffer, Ph.D.
University of Strathclyde
Glasgow, Scotland

A Changing Role for Dad

Today, there is no such thing as an average father. Family organization and sex roles are shifting so rapidly that a father's role can no longer be rigidly defined. In fact, if anything, fathers are increasingly throwing off the traditional mantle of the distanced authoritarian figure and taking an active hand in the raising of their youngsters. The reasons for this are various, but three stand out and have to do with birthing, new economic circumstances, and the rapidly increasing numbers of divorces and subsequent remarriages.

The dramatic increase in caesarean-section deliveries, for example, has led many fathers to assume larger parental responsibilities in the days just following the birth as the mothers recover from surgery. Psychologists have noted that the majority of fathers who accept these early responsibilities acquire a greater personal involvement with their infants than fathers who leave most parenting duties to the mothers.

The sharp increase in working mothers has also done much to change the picture. Between 1950 and 1987, for example, the employment rate more than quadrupled for married mothers of preschoolers. As a result, fathers have had to assume more duties at home, including housework and child care.

Another major influence on the way fathers respond to their children has been the changing nature of many men's jobs. New occupations and economic need have taken fathers away from small businesses and farms where they worked in proximity to their families. Today, more and more men commute to jobs far from home. Whereas once their mere presence was enough to automatically ensure them a role in the day-to-day life of the family, they must now consciously strive for an effective place. Paternity leave, flexible working hours, and a shorter work week are innovations that have helped some men to achieve the goal of being more fully engaged with their children.

Fathers, it turns out, can be as involved with or interested in their children as mothers. Studies have shown that fathers of new babies are just as competent as mothers in caregiving but tend to spend more of their time with their infants in play rather than in practical duties of parenthood.

Unfortunately, at the very moment when the fathering role is enlarging, various negative forces are emerging. Over the last decade, the dramatic rise in the rates of separation and divorce has, in many cases, lessened opportunities for fathers to exercise their talents as parents. Fortunately, the old presumption that maternal custody is always in the best interests of the child is changing. A man's competence as parent and caregiver is increasingly being recognized by the courts as more and more fathers seek joint custody or full-time custody of their children. Although only a small percentage of fathers have been given custody, so far the evidence indicates that youngsters do at least as well living with the father as with the mother, and in the case of sons, they may even do slightly better.

Ross D. Parke, Ph.D.
University of Illinois
Champaign, Illinois

A broadening of gender roles

Fortunately for today's children, parents can offer a greater range of possibilities for gender identification than was true a generation or so ago. Mother is no longer expected to stay home, clean, cook, and care for children to the exclusion of her need for personal expression. Nor does she have to conceal her sports ability, spirit of adventure, aggressiveness, or business acumen, which once were viewed as unfeminine traits. By the same token, the father has become less of a remote member of the family circle and is more likely to function as an equal partner in home and child care, especially when his wife has a full-time job. And in an age when feelings may be openly displayed, he can be affectionate and demonstrative, showing his tears as well as his joys. With this broadening of gender roles, sons and daughters can stretch themselves, becoming more rounded human beings in the process. ❖

How Unalike Are Boys and Girls?

Boys and girls behave differently from one another: true or false? Few parents would hesitate to answer "true." Quite apart from their anatomical differences, young children do seem to have many emotional and social traits that most people associate with gender.

But are these differences real? If they are real, are they biologically determined or learned? Do parents teach these sex-role traits by treating their children differently—or do they treat their children differently in response to inborn factors that make a girl's aptitudes and preferences different from a boy's?

The one answer to all these questions, according to the latest studies, is "both." Some measurable differences between the sexes do exist in early childhood, as shown on these pages. The physical differences are biological; many of the behavioral differences are probably learned. Some favorite notions about the differences between boys and girls do not hold up under scrutiny and must be dismissed as myths and stereotypes.

For instance, everyone knows boys are stronger than girls—but what is meant by "strong?" While boys are taller, more muscular, and more active at birth than girls, girls in fact are less vulnerable than boys to injury and disease at birth—and before birth—and all through childhood.

In view of the debate about the differences, the real surprise in the research is that, all in all, boys and girls are more alike than not; the

What Little Boys Are Really Made Of

- Boys are taller, heavier, and more muscular; they lose baby fat sooner.

- Boys have slightly more muscle strength than girls of equal size; but boys suffer more prenatal problems, birth injuries, and childhood diseases.

- Boys are usually superior to girls in large-muscle skills by four or five.

- Boys engage in more aggression than girls do and express it physically and verbally.

- Boys' self-esteem is often based on their physical abilities.

- Boys have more energy than girls do, play in larger groups, and engage in more active, rough play.

- Boys try harder than girls do to dominate adults and one another.

- Boys are as dependent, emotional, and empathetic as girls.

differences detected are in very small margins. But a part of every child's task in becoming part of the community is to develop a secure gender identity and learn the behaviors that go with it; and part of a parent's task is to help teach them. Long before they understand that gender is permanent or that it has to do with reproduction, children eagerly assert, "I'm a boy!" and "Girls don't hit!" Their fierce insistence on sex-typed behaviors is a way of making sense of their world.

Some of the facts in the adjacent charts may be startling. These findings represent averages, based on studies with large numbers of children six and younger. And while the averages differ—often by only a percentage point or two—the groups overlap, each group containing some children who exceed the averages for the other sex.

Many girls, for instance, can jump farther than the average boy their age, although greater physical strength is usually attributed to boys; and many boys talk before the average girl, although girls are assumed to be more verbal. Thus, when a father fears that his son is insufficiently masculine because he does not see him engaging in the same rough, aggressive play as boys in general, he is forgetting that behind that majority of roughnecks is a large minority of normal boys who are temperamentally quiet, just like his son.

What Little Girls Are Really Made Of

- Girls play in smaller groups; less susceptible to peer pressure.

- Girls have greater verbal ability, using complex sentences earlier.

- Girls outdo boys at some small-muscle tasks by four or five.

- Girls are more affectionate and nurturing to younger children.

- Girls value achievement as mastery, not as a competitive victory.

- Girls express their aggression socially; they may ignore a newcomer or deny requested help.

- Girls' self-esteem equals boys', but it is based on social rather than physical competence.

- Girls are equal to boys in mathematical and analytical abilities.

- Girls at birth are physiologically more mature; they lose their baby teeth earlier; their brains specialize—e.g., for language, sooner.

Genetics and Your Child

Who your child is and what kind of person she will become greatly depend on the genetic inheritance you and your partner have bequeathed her. Not only, of course, was her sex determined at the moment of conception through the union of egg and sperm, but also such traits as her eye color, the size and tilt of her nose, her future height, and to a surprising extent, her intelligence and even her temperament. Naturally your child's development will be shaped and modified by the manner in which you raise her and by various environmental influences, many beyond your control; but the genes you both gave her will always remain the same, joining her to you and other members of the family and at the same time setting her apart as one of a kind—her own special self.

Once a mystery, the fascinating process by which a human being acquires a unique genetic identity is now clearly understood. Inherited traits are passed from parent to child on chromosomes—long, threadlike strands of a chemical sequence known as deoxyribonucleic acid, or DNA. Found in the nuclei of all human cells, these DNA strands are shaped like spiral staircases. Each "step" is composed of a group of DNA molecules and forms a gene, a basic unit of coded information that fixes individual traits.

Human cells normally contain forty-six chromosomes, arranged in twenty-three pairs. Exceptions to the rule are the sex cells—the male sperm cell and the female ovum, or egg—which have only half the full number of chromosomes, or twenty-three. At conception, the twenty-three chromosomes of the sperm cell join with the twenty-three of the ovum to form a new fertilized cell, or zygote, with forty-six chromosomes in all. Thus, each parent makes an equal contribution to the genetic makeup of their baby.

Scientists have identified and numbered all twenty-three pairs of human chromosomes. The twenty-third pair, the sex chromosomes, consists of two chromosomes called XX (because of their shape) in the female and an X and Y in the male. The sex of a child depends on which sex chromosomes unite during fertilization. Thus, while the mother always contributes an X, the father contributes either an X or a Y, and this determines whether the child will be XX, a girl, or XY, a boy.

Although all children in a family acquire half of their genetic inheritance from each parent, the genes that each child receives are astonishingly varied. One sibling may be stout and another thin, one shy, another outgoing, or one chronically ill and another abundantly healthy. These individual differences are due in part to the fact that no two sperm or egg cells contain the same arrangement of genes. During fertilization, the twenty-three chromsome pairs of the male sperm cell and of the female egg join to form an entirely new combination of genes for each trait. With tens of thousands of different genes on each chromosome, the number of possible rearrangements is staggering. Excluding identical twins, who originate from the same fertilized egg, the odds of two children having matching genetic makeups are next to impossible.

Still, enough like genes are inherited by siblings to establish some common traits among them. Children born of the same parents often have similar coloring and physiques and display the same manner of talking or walking—even when they are raised apart. They are also likely to have similar IQs and, to a lesser extent, possess many of the same talents. These traits are often passed on through several generations. The Darwin family, for example, produced five generations of renowned scientists. But genius can crop up unexpectedly. The right combination of DNA molecules can yield extraordinarily talented offspring, even when the parents themselves are not particularly gifted, as evidenced by the births of Albert Einstein and William Shakespeare.

No matter what a child's genetic inheritance may be, the youngster remains subject to external influences, so that, depending on circumstance, the potential first violinist may wind up a first baseman instead. A gift almost always has to be developed for it to blossom. Even physical characteristics, which are under strict genetic control, can be altered by environmental factors. A youngster fed a poor diet while growing up may not reach her genetically programmed height. Thus, despite genetics' sway, your child's physical, emotional, and intellectual development still depends largely on you—and on the love and care you are able to provide during the formative years of her life.

Within almost every human cell are twenty-three pairs of chromosomes, the carriers of heredity. Twenty-two pairs are identical. The twenty-third pair, which distinguishes sex, is dissimilar—XY in males (left), XX in females (right).

Chromosomes from the father are passed through a sperm cell (above) to the mother's egg (right). Each contains half—twenty-three—of the parent's set of paired chromosomes.

Chromosomes from both parents combine in the fertilized egg cell (left). With the union of two X chromosomes, a girl results, and various traits are laid down. Each trait-causing gene has a specific location on the chromosomes. Here, in the fertilized egg, the gene for the piebald, or white forelock, trait is borne on chromosome pair number four (circled).

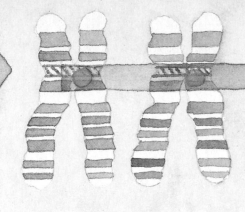

Because the piebald gene (circles) is dominant, a child need receive it from only one parent in order for the white forelock to show up in her hair.

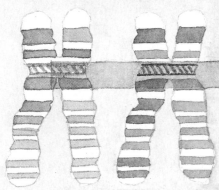

The piebald gene is absent from the chromosomes at left. The child with these chromosomes inherits instead two dark-haired genes and, as a result, will have dark hair only.

The Indelible Stamp of Genes

In the pairing of chromosomes that occurs when sperm fertilizes egg, the various inborn traits that make an individual unique become fixed. When two dissimilar genes unite, one has the capacity to block the other and keep it from having its effect. The stronger gene is called dominant; the weaker gene is said to be recessive—that is, the trait it encapsulates will not show up in the child, but may emerge in the next or a future generation when paired with another recessive gene.

The striking feature of a white forelock, known as the piebald trait, is an example of a dominant gene asserting itself; when paired with a gene for dark hair, it always exerts its influence. Thus, a child who inherits the piebald gene from one parent and a dark-hair gene from the other will be born with the white streak. The gene apparently produces the streak by interfering with the formation of the pigment that normally would color the hair.

Occasionally, one gene may incompletely dominate another, and the result is a blend of traits. For example, a child who inherits a dominant curly-haired gene from one parent and a recessive straight-haired gene from the other may end up with wavy hair. In addition, many traits result from a mixture of several genes (multigene). The shape and size of your child's nose, for example, is determined by just such a mix, although genes for large noses tend to dominate over genes for smaller ones.

Physically Inherited Traits

Various human physical traits are listed here under two headings: Dominant and Recessive. Dominant genes often block recessive ones, but when two recessive genes are paired, their trait emerges. Thus, though a child inherits an equal number of chromosomes from each parent, she may resemble one more than the other.

Dominant	Recessive
Hair	
Dark	Blond
Other hair color	Red
Curly	Straight
Early baldness (dominant in males)	Normal
Widow's peak	Straight hairline
White forelock	Normal coloration
Abundant on body	Little on body
Skin	
Freckles	Lack of freckles
Pigmented skin, hair, eyes	Albinism
Black skin	White skin
Mouth	
Broad lips	Thin lips
Ability to roll tongue	Inability to roll tongue
Dimples	Dimples absent
Eyes	
Brown iris	Blue or gray iris
Hazel or green iris	Blue or gray iris

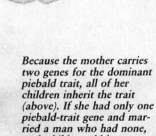

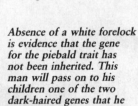

A striking white forelock signals the presence of the gene for the piebald trait. In this instance, the woman inherited it from both parents and carries two genes for the trait.

Absence of a white forelock is evidence that the gene for the piebald trait has not been inherited. This man will pass on to his children one of the two dark-haired genes that he received from his parents.

Because the mother carries two genes for the dominant piebald trait, all of her children inherit the trait (above). If she had only one piebald-trait gene and married a man who had none, each child would have a fifty-fifty chance of exhibiting the piebald trait.

Dominant	**Recessive**
Large eyes	Small eyes
Epicanthic fold	No fold
Ears	
Free ear lobes	Attached ear lobes
Nose	
Roman	Straight
Broad nostrils	Narrow nostrils
High, narrow bridge	Low, narrow bridge
Hands	
Hitchhiker's (backward bending) thumb	Straight thumb
Little finger bent inward	Little finger straight
Second finger shorter than fourth	Second finger longer than fourth
Hair on midfinger	Lack of hair
Blood type	
A	O
B	O
AB	O
Rh positive	Rh negative

When Genes Go Awry

Scientists estimate that every human being carries between three and eight genes on his or her chromosomes that are capable of producing diseases or handicaps. Most of these genes are recessive and therefore have no effect on the person who possesses only one of them, since the gene is then effectively masked by a dominant gene. But this same individual can pass such a gene on to half of his children. In the rare event that two people with similar harmful recessive genes get married, each of their children will then have a 25 percent chance of inheriting both genes and

thus of acquiring one of the genetically caused conditions that are listed in the chart on the opposite page.

A few genetic disorders are carried by a dominant rather than a recessive gene. In such cases, the carrier of the defective gene is afflicted with the disease and each child born to the carrier has a 50 percent chance of having it too—or a 75 percent chance if both of the parents are carriers.

Sometimes a genetic disorder is not inherited, but arises when the structure or number of chromosomes or a section of DNA in a developing sperm or egg cell changes, or mutates. Most mutations

occur for unknown reasons, although exposure to X-rays, high temperatures, and certain toxic chemicals are recognized as contributing causes.

There are certain other genetic disorders that arise from the presence of an abnormal number of chromosomes. The form of mental retardation known as Down syndrome, for example, occurs when chromosomes fail to pair properly during cell division to create the sex cells. As a result, the child receives an extra chromosome at the twenty-first pair of chromosomes and is thus fated to be born with the condition.

Sex-Linked Disorders

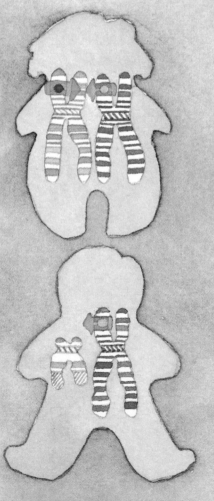

Recessive genes for certain disorders, such as muscular dystrophy, hemophilia, and color blindness, are located on the female sex chromosome (X) and are referred to as sex-linked. A girl who receives one of these genes from a parent does not inherit the disorder because she also receives a corresponding— and dominant—normal gene from her other parent.

In a family where the mother carries a gene for a sex-linked disorder, only a son will be affected. This is because the Y chromosome (far left), which is one-third smaller than the X chromosome, carries no corresponding gene to block the trait. An afflicted male can pass on a gene that causes the disorder to his daughter, who will become a carrier but will not develop the disorder herself because she has a corresponding dominant gene to mask the trait.

Genes' Heavy Toll

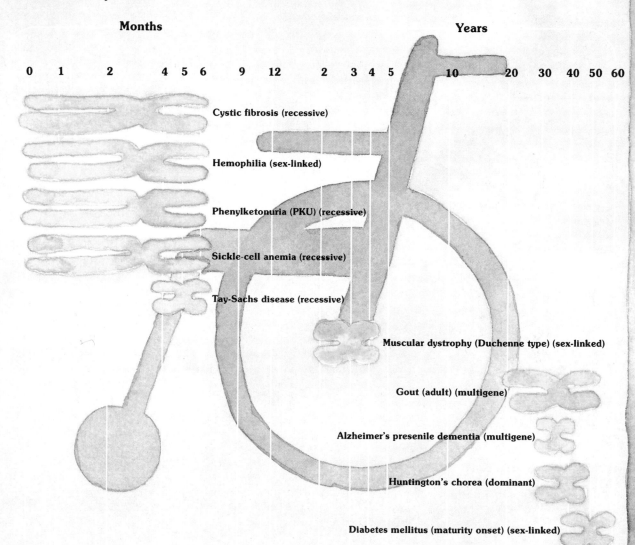

Months

Years

0   1   2   4 5 6   9   12   2   3 4 5   10   20   30 40 50 60

Cystic fibrosis (recessive)

Hemophilia (sex-linked)

Phenylketonuria (PKU) (recessive)

Sickle-cell anemia (recessive)

Tay-Sachs disease (recessive)

Muscular dystrophy (Duchenne type) (sex-linked)

Gout (adult) (multigene)

Alzheimer's presenile dementia (multigene)

Huntington's chorea (dominant)

Diabetes mellitus (maturity onset) (sex-linked)

Nature vs. Nurture

Your child's basic temperament—whether impulsive or reflective, sunny or withdrawn—is partially determined by inherited traits, some of which yield more to molding by environmental factors than others. Many scientists now believe that at least half of a child's personality is shaped by heredity.

Studies have shown that leadership qualities are 61 percent inherited, while the need for intimacy is only 33 percent inherited. Among other highly inherita-

ble traits are creativity, conformity, and the tendency to worry (*chart, opposite, top*). This is not to say that a shy child cannot be encouraged to become more outgoing, or a worrier helped to feel more secure about things.

The genetic base of intelligence has also been demonstrated. Studies have shown that the more closely two people are related, the higher the correlation between their IQs. Biological siblings, for example, usually score closer on IQ

tests than do adopted siblings. Nevertheless, genes are by no means the sole factor in determining intellect. Parental input and support, along with good schooling, make a major contribution. Birth order and stability in the home also play important roles. Firstborn children and children whose families are stable often have a better chance of realizing their potential than their siblings or those youngsters who have been set back by family problems.

Environment's Varying Influence

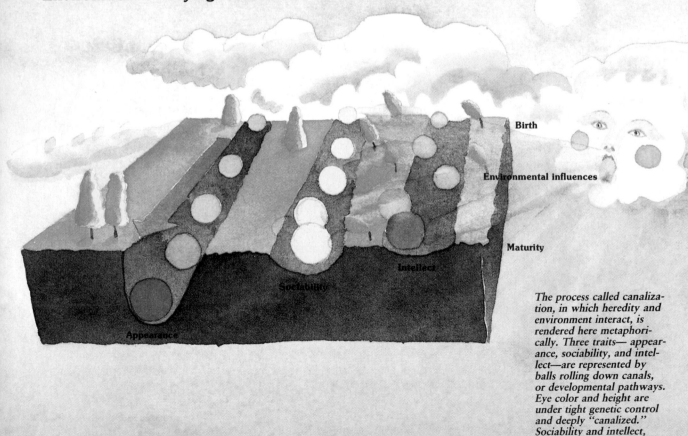

Birth

Environmental influences

Maturity

Intellect

Sociability

Appearance

The process called canalization, in which heredity and environment interact, is rendered here metaphorically. Three traits— appearance, sociability, and intellect—are represented by balls rolling down canals, or developmental pathways. Eye color and height are under tight genetic control and deeply "canalized." Sociability and intellect, which follow shallower paths, are more susceptible to the "winds" of environmental influences.

A Spectrum of Modifiable Traits

The chart at right shows the relationship between genetic inheritance and environment for eleven personality traits as revealed by a study. Previously, most scientists did not think that inheritance was such a factor in influencing many of these traits.

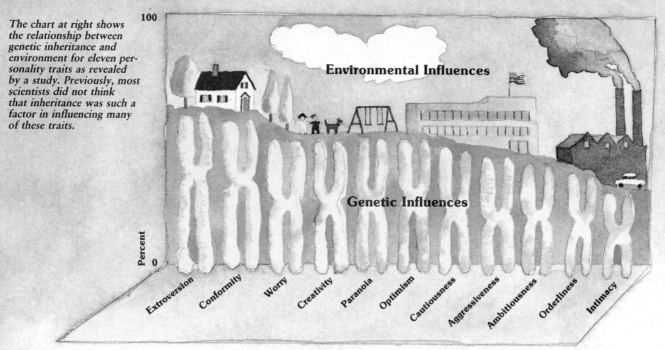

Environmental Influences

Genetic Influences

100

Percent

0

Extroversion · Conformity · Worry · Creativity · Paranoia · Optimism · Cautiousness · Aggressiveness · Ambitiousness · Orderliness · Intimacy

Reaching for Potential

This diagram shows how environment affects intellect. If four youngsters of differing potential are raised in an unstimulating milieu, the one with the greatest ability (Child A) will suffer most. But when he is reared in a stimulating environment, he is likely to realize his fullest potential because he has what the scientists call the broadest reaction range, or capacity to respond to stimuli.

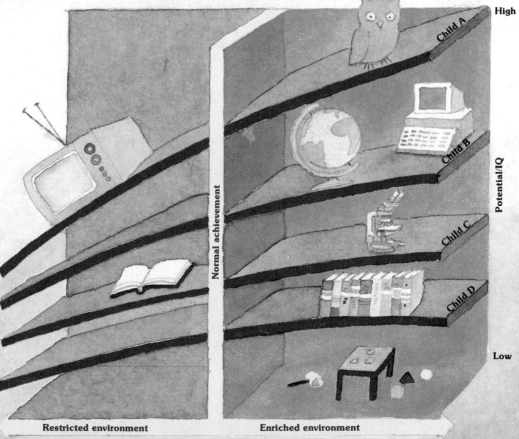

High

Child A

Child B

Child C

Child D

Potential/IQ

Normal achievement

Low

Restricted environment

Enriched environment

Social and Emotional Development

It is a relatively new notion to think of a child as a continually evolving social being, a notion defined and explored by the science called developmental psychology. An underlying premise of this discipline is that just as a youngster's body grows in predictable ways, so her social and emotional development follow certain natural progressions. Like gains in weight or height, social and emotional growth are simple to observe. They are immediately reflected in the child's day-to-day activities.

With each new development, parents and child must readjust the terms of their relationship. Parents, who begin as the essential center of their offspring's lives, gradually cease being all things to their children. Instead, parents have to guide their youngsters to ever-greater self-control and self-reliance. The child must likewise give up her dependency and gradually replace it with autonomy and responsibility. Children also have to make internal adjustments, revising their self-estimates upward or downward as the situation requires. When they are able to deal with the demands of their expanding world, they can continue on an upward cycle, feeling good about their abilities and being eager for greater challenges, and parents should encourage them in this as much as possible. There will also be times when a youngster's ambitions outstrip her abilities, and she is forced to take a somewhat diminished view of herself. During these periods the child requires extra doses of parental support and responsiveness.

A child's individual evolution occurs in four broad stages. At first, when she is an infant, her basic social and emotional tasks involve developing basic trust in her parents and a deep attachment to them. Once these crucial ties to mother and father are made, they serve as a base for all future social and emotional growth.

On this foundation the toddler, who has learned to walk and gained the independence mobility confers, begins to build self-esteem and to recognize her own individuality. She investigates and explores, discovering in the process the wide range of her abilities.

The preschooler, three and four years old, forges her way into a wider social and emotional realm. She identifies with her parents and imitates them as she begins to master skills such as empathy, sharing, and obedience to rules. These new abilities enable her to get along with people beyond her immediate family.

The kindergartner, five years old, makes a place for herself in the larger social sphere of school. She is old enough to comfort and nurture younger children. She also develops a more mature sense of her own identity and, for the first time, understands the concept of time. She sees herself as a person with a past, a present, and a future.

Through these developmental advances the youngster learns to live in a community—first fitting into the community of her family, then expanding outward. In this process of social and emotional learning, the parents are the most influential teachers. It is they who help the child acquire social skills and inner values. It is they who steadily improve the self-control necessary for living in the wider world.

The path to maturity is often rocky, but being aware of your child's developmental level will make living

together easier for everyone. For example, if you are ready for such changes as the fear of strangers that will appear at eight to ten months of age, the signs of anxiety will seem not just tolerable, but positive, because they are an indication of growth. According to developmental psychologists, the appearance of stranger anxiety shows that your baby has a brand-new ability to compare past experiences with those of the present. For the first time, the child realizes that a stranger's face is different from your face or from the faces of other members of the family. Unable at first to make sense of what he sees, he grows wary. Later, when he has more ability to relate the unfamiliar to things that he does know, this kind of anxiety will diminish.

It is also useful to know when an older child is likely to acquire new skills—and to realize that no amount of instruction or cajoling is going to accelerate the process. For instance, a skill such as sharing is extremely desirable, but it is not within the capabilities of an infant. To be able to share, a youngster has to make several cognitive advances. For one thing, he has to learn that objects are permanent—that they do not cease to exist just because they are out of sight. The child also has to learn that there is a future, and that the favorite toy that he gives to a playmate can come back to him eventually. Only with this knowledge is he capable of sharing gracefully. In the meantime, you must look at the resolute way he clutches a toy as a healthy sign of growing self-awareness.

In fact, greedy possessiveness, which is one step along the path to sharing, is one of many less-than-attractive behaviors that are forerunners of new social skills. While you should react to antisocial behavior and encourage acceptable conduct, you also should recall that even undesirable behaviors play a role in development.

For example, some parents are alarmed the first time they hear their preschooler exaggerate to the point of lying. But a child's tall tales may be nothing more than the exercise of newfound imagination. Even an outright lie—such as when he blames an invisible friend for a messy spill—may be nothing

more than the youngster's way of testing his understanding of his own identity. It is perfectly valid for you to look at a three-year-old's experiments with deception as stepping-stones to greater maturity.

Even tantrums, which are among the most difficult behaviors to keep in perspective, can be seen as evidence of growth. A two-year-old expressing rage through a tantrum may be frustrated because his ambitions have temporarily outdistanced his abilities. To get himself into such a fix in the first place, he has to have a growing sense of his own powers and a willingness to put them to the test.

The socialization process is gradual, and the child develops in many different ways at once. From a practical standpoint, however, it is useful to know that each of the broad stages of social development embraces a distinct collection of physical, mental, emotional, and social skills and behaviors.

The chart that follows divides the years from birth to the age of six into four developmental stages—infancy, toddlerhood, preschool, and kindergarten. The bulleted lists that make up the chart trace the progress of a child's emotional development and outline the order in which she acquires the social skills that shape her relationship to her family and to the outside world. As you consult the chart, bear in mind that the boundaries between stages are necessarily blurry. Behaviors from each stage gradually fade out, as those of the succeeding stage come to predominate. Because the dividing lines between stages are not hard and fast, you can expect your child to move ahead of schedule in some areas and lag behind in others. The developments described for each stage are only the norms—averages derived from the study of many children. They are not a rigid timetable for your child.

Infants

Your newborn baby is a vulnerable, disorganized bundle of needs, but he does possess a certain instinctual knack for getting those needs met. Even his less appealing behavior—the crying, fussing, and waking up at all hours of the night—causes you to engage in rudimentary communication, calling your attention to his wants. And he is quick to develop more graceful methods of engaging your attention. Within a few weeks he learns to smile, to gurgle, to gaze raptly at your face, to snuggle in your arms and coo contentedly.

For the first three months or so, the infant accepts care and comfort from almost anyone. But as he matures and becomes accustomed to the fact that you are particularly responsive to him, he comes to rely on you. At two to three months he reacts differently to you than to other people. He cries less when you are near, and he smiles and babbles more readily. He is also more easily consoled by you than by anyone else. By six or seven months, he is profoundly attached to you. He is becoming a full-fledged member of the family.

Relationship with Parents

- By about two months, moves limbs excitedly at sight of parents or sound of their voices.

- By about four months, smiles, reaches and "talks" more to people who are familiar than to strangers.

- By six or seven months, lifts arms to parents in greeting; begins to show strong attachment to parents, seeking to stay close to them and be comforted only by them.

- By seven months, is distressed when parent leaves the room.

- By eight months or so, shows trust in parents by turning confidently to them for comfort in distress.

- Around ten months, says "dada" or "mama."

- By the end of this period, likes to be within sight and hearing of parents constantly; does not like to be alone and may be troubled when left with strangers or in the care of a baby-sitter.

- By one year, is clearly attached to parents and, perhaps, to one or two other people, such as grandparents or caregiver.

Relationship with Siblings

- As early as six months, distinguishes siblings from other people; may wiggle excitedly to acknowledge their presence.

- By seven to eight months, plays peekaboo and other simple games with a cooperative older brother or older sister.

- By ten months, begins to interact with a sibling by holding on to a contested toy or crawling away.

- At twelve months, often has formed attachments to siblings, greeting them enthusiastically and taking comfort in their attention.

- By end of period, plays happily alongside his siblings, although he does not really play with them yet.

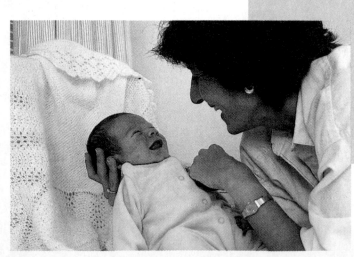

Sense of Self

- By four months, smiles at any image in a mirror, without yet recognizing himself; begins to distinguish his own mirror image at about seven months.

- By six months, will protest vocally and grasp objects more tightly when an adult or sibling tries to take them away.

- As early as seven months, may respond to hearing own name; at around nine months, turns head, makes eye contact, and smiles at the person speaking.

Social Skills

- From birth, cries to get attention and has distinctly different cries to express different needs or to signal fear, disgust, or anger; develops facial expressions to convey these feelings by about five months.

- From birth, enjoys watching people, concentrating on faces and eyes; seeks physical contact.

- Approaching first birthday, is sensitive to other children and may cry when another child cries.

- By first birthday, hugs and kisses; waves good-bye.

- By first birthday, repeats acts that make parents smile or laugh.

Parents' Role

Predictable daily routines are particularly important during the first few months, when the baby's main task is to regulate his body rhythms and gain stability. Be prompt in meeting his basic needs—food, sleep, warmth, and cuddling. In doing so, you earn his trust right from the start.

During the remainder of the first year, your sensitive, reliable responses to his cries help him cope with frustration and helplessness. By warmly enjoying your baby, you nourish the bond that develops between you.

Toddlers

A toddler's trademark changeability has a way of throwing parents off stride. Just as the mother and father have gotten comfortable caring for a needful infant, the youngster abruptly begins the transformation into an independent person. She wants her parents to let go a little, to give her some elbowroom. But she also wants them to be there and waiting, should anything go wrong.

From the child's perspective, it is at once a wonderful and frightening time. She is never quite certain what surprises await her and never really knows whether she can master the challenges she undertakes. Whatever the risks might be, she wants to try.

When she fails, as she often must, the frustration can be overwhelming. She may become temporarily more dependent on you or rely on comfort rituals, such as thumb-sucking and blanket-clutching. She may also give vent to her frustration in an occasional temper tantrum. From her parents she needs patience, support, and a bit of protection from attempting too much and failing too often. Gaining greater self-confidence and self-esteem is what the toddler's advances and retreats are all about.

Relationship with Parents

- Throughout this period, grows increasingly content to explore and play independently, as long as parent is in the same room.

- Continues to be distressed by real separations from parents and even after four to six months of walking, is strongly dependent on parents; needs to know where they are every minute, follows them about, reaches for a hand in unfamiliar surroundings.

- Often says "no" and is sometimes balky in following instructions.

- Uses new language skills to call out to parents and ask for whatever she needs or wants.

- In play, imitates adult activities— cleaning the house, raking the yard, washing the car—modeling self on parents' actions.

- By the middle of this period, likes to show affection; spontaneously hugs and kisses parents.

- After second birthday, grows less absorbed with her own needs and develops more of a feeling of partnership with parents; in some instances, understands their simpler needs—may, for example, agree to wait for a snack while parent finishes a task.

Relationship with Siblings

- Likes rough-and-tumble play with older siblings.

- By eighteen months, may show signs of jealousy when brother or sister gets attention—may, for example, push her way into the middle of a game that a parent is playing with one of her siblings.

- By two years old, imitates older siblings in such activities as playing and reading, and in the ways that they show their emotions.

- May sometimes try to comfort a sibling who is hurt or upset, by bringing a toy, fetching an adult to help, or stroking the other child affectionately.

- By the end of this period, can sometimes cooperate in games and play with older siblings without parental supervision.

Sense of Self

- Begins doing things for self that adults had done for him before, such as feeding self, dressing, and turning pages of a book.

- Around eighteen months of age, displays budding self-esteem and confidence with expressions such as "Me do it."

- May pick up and put away toys when asked, especially if consistently praised for efforts.

- May claim and defend ownership of possessions, sometimes doing so aggressively.

- Around second birthday, begins calling self by name; by three years, can give her full name if asked.

- Becomes aware of gender differences though not understanding that the differences are lifelong.

- Takes pride in her achievements and, beyond two-and-a-half, increasingly wants to do things on her own.

Social Skills

- Talks in simple one- or two-word sentences, as spoken vocabulary grows to hundreds of words; can follow simple instructions, such as "Bring me your cup."

- At eighteen months, generally wants to play near other children rather than with them.

- At two-and-a-half, plays alongside children of same age, in similar or even imitative activities, but without actually taking part in their games.

- Tries to give comfort as she has been comforted; uses phrases such as "kiss and make better."

- Enjoys wide range of relationships with relatives and family friends; is comfortable meeting new people, especially when parents are nearby.

- Nearing third birthday, resists change in routines such as meal or nap schedules or in her bedtime rituals; needs much reassurance.

- Can begin to participate in simple group activities such as circle games, clapping games, dances.

Parents' Role

From twelve to eighteen months is a time of rapidly expanding exploration, but your toddler needs to know that you are there should she ever need to retreat. From eighteen months on, she requires continued encouragement, but you should offer to help now only if she asks you to. Be subtle in guiding her to challenges you know she can master.

You must also set consistent limits on behavior. Diplomatically but firmly show your toddler that you expect cooperation and require obedience.

Preschoolers

Sometime around his third birthday, a child turns more attention to the world outside the home. He still loves his parents and clings to their familiar ways of doing things, but he is ready for broader experiences. Though leaving the "terrible twos" behind, he still struggles to capture a sense of independence and begins to find it in the company of his peers.

Much of his learning now occurs through play—with peers and parents, or all by himself with the friends and foes he supplies through imagination. The play is fun, certainly, but it also is a testing ground in which he discovers how people get along.

With boundless energy, he refines his skills in many different directions all at the same time. His gender identification also deepens and by the time he starts kindergarten, he shows a marked preference for spending time with same-sex companions and for the typical interests and activities of boys.

Relationship with Parents

- At three years, finds it easier to say "yes" and is less likely to resist parents' wishes.

- Around three-and-a-half, may be able to separate from parent easily and without protest when dropped off at nursery school or at the home of a friend.

- May feel passionate fondness for parents, especially the parent of the opposite sex.

- Is adjusting to parents' expectations about social behavior; says "please" and "thank you," though perhaps not consistently.

Relationship with Siblings

- Shows affection for younger brothers and sisters by giving them hugs and kisses.

- By four years of age, usually shows concern when siblings are hurt or unhappy; as they approach five years old, girls tend to exhibit more of this nurturing behavior than boys.

- May assume the role of a "little adult" in protecting, entertaining, and teaching a baby brother or baby sister.

- Plays with siblings intensely and often; in most families with two or more children, may spend more time with siblings than with either mother or father.

- Increasingly shows preference for sex-typed activities—dolls for girls, trucks for boys; begins to seek playmates of the same sex.

- At three years of age, begins to identify own feelings such as love, hate, sadness, and fear; gradually learns to talk about these feelings.

- Sometimes creates imaginary companions; may assign the role of the rebellious alter ego to such a "friend," chastising it for his own unacceptable behavior.

- May become private and modest about undressing and using the bathroom.

- Likes to perform and entertain others; wants to call attention to self.

- Defines self in physical terms—"I'm a boy who can play ball"—rather than in terms of personality traits.

- Learns to control some negative impulses; will sometimes use aggressive play or words in situations where he once resorted to physical violence.

- Becomes more sensitive to others' feelings; at four-and-a-half or five, may notice when another child is angry or scared.

- Looks to peers for good and bad models of social interaction.

- Has broader range of interaction with peers—sharing, playing games, talking, cooperating, imitating; but also exhibits more negative interplay, such as hitting, grabbing, and quarreling.

- Typically prefers company of one child at a time; may become bossy or sulky when a third child joins in.

- Uses language effectively to socialize, persuade, or share information.

Parents' Role

As the child's world broadens, you are still the prime teachers, but you are joined by other influences—among them playmates, nursery-school teachers, and television. Clear and consistent rules are all the more important. Enforce them in a warm, loving way that is at the same time firm. As your child seeks increasingly to act on his own, remember that he is best served by learning self-control. That lesson is best transmitted through praise and encouragement of appropriate behavior.

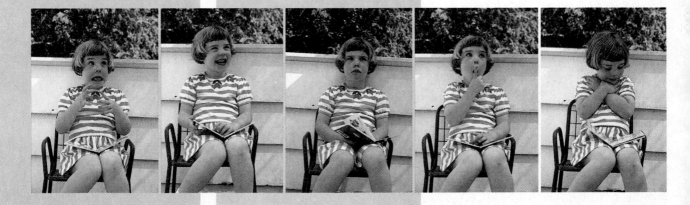

35

Kindergartners

The year between the fifth and sixth birthdays is a very satisfying time for most youngsters and their parents. The five-year-old seems to have everything going for her. She loves her home and family, she feels comfortable with her peers, and has such a good grasp of language that she can say just about anything she needs to. She also has a pretty good idea of who she is and has developed the self-control to begin meeting your standards for behavior.

The five-year-old also has acquired an understanding of time. She remembers the past and can make plans for the future. At this age, she usually enjoys planned changes much more than sudden surprises. She thrives on fulfilling her familiar routines.

Kindergarten is the ideal place for her now. Her intellectual abilities are growing, and she is ready for the transition to a more structured learning environment. With confidence rooted in the emotional backing of her family, she will thrive upon the varied new challenges of her school experience.

Relationship with Parents

- Shows affection to both parents; wants to please them most of the time.

- May respond more readily to father's discipline and control than to mother's.

- Imitates parent of the same sex, particularly in play.

- Carries out simple chores at home with parents' supervision.

Relationship with Siblings

- Usually treats younger sibling well; girls are especially likely to be helpful and protective, and to mimic their mothers in words and manner when dealing with children who are smaller.

- Though caring, is still not capable of shouldering much responsibility for a younger sibling because her attention span is limited, and she is still quite immature in controlling her emotions.

- At times, is now able to express anger toward siblings verbally rather than physically.

Sense of Self

- Likes to feel grown-up; boasts about own superiority to younger, less capable children.

- At the same time, begins to develop a more realistic sense of own personal qualities by comparing self to other children in kindergarten.

- Shows determination to get own way, to follow through on plans, and to win arguments, but usually does so with newfound self-control and poise.

- Begins to base decisions on a sense of right and wrong, rather than on fear of being punished.

Social Skills

- Can learn to understand the feelings of others through simple role-playing.

- Will play contentedly and independently in the homes of friends, with as little as an hourly check by an adult.

- Accepts idea of taking turns and of recognizing a winner.

- Understands and respects rules; often asks permission, especially at school.

- Understands and enjoys both giving and receiving; may still have a shaky sense of ownership, however, and may give away or take things that are not her own.

Parents' Role

When your child starts kindergarten, her horizons widen. To share in her excitement over school, make time to discuss each day's events. Examine the work that she brings home and praise her to show that you value her efforts. Continue to promote helpful and caring behavior. When you set limits, do it in such a way that you always make it clear that you are criticizing the youngster's actions, not the child herself. In this way you preserve her conviction that she can do better.

Birth of a Family

It is a scene rich in poignance and ritual. A pregnant young woman sits on the bed with her husband, packing an overnight case. They are preparing for the trip to the hospital. A new life is about to begin—and with it the birth of a family.

The arrival of the first child brings fundamental changes. What has been a couple—two individuals with their own concerns and romantic preoccupations—suddenly is transformed into something profoundly different. Two become three. The needs of the family now take first priority.

Although such new threesomes are as various as the individuals who constitute them and the circumstances that have shaped them, all of them share certain phases and tasks characterizing the process that marks the formation of a family.

First comes the momentous transition to parenthood. Both husband and wife are entering a new stage in their lives, one fundamentally different from those that have gone before. Now they must think first not of themselves, but of the welfare of another human being. The time frame that begins with pregnancy and extends through the first year or two of the child's life is packed with new experiences, hitherto unknown stresses, and enormous rewards. Parents must learn to cope with the round-the-clock demands of their newborn while simultaneously readjusting their own relationship and laying the financial groundwork for the family's future security. Then, having successfully progressed through this intense period of transition, they enter a new phase of family planning. They must decide whether one youngster is enough and, if not, how soon to add another child to the family. This section traces the ups and downs of parenthood and suggests how you can take some of the pressures off yourself as you cope day by day, and at the same time look ahead to the future.

A Transition of Joys and Trials

For most young parents, the initial months and years of their first child's life are, despite thronging uncertainties and disruptions, a time of great happiness. Most parents derive deep satisfaction simply from the realization that they are needed by another human—and needed as they never have been before. Parents often have a sense that they themselves are growing, drawing on previously untapped reservoirs of energy and resourcefulness. And then there is the transcendent reward of seeing such a small, dependent being thrive and grow and begin to interact with them and with the world around her.

To watch the unfolding of a brand-new personality, quite different in its blend of traits from any other one on earth, is perhaps most rewarding and enthralling of all.

Nurturing a new life nevertheless involves a great deal of trouble and work. Having a little one in the home shatters the relative calm of a traditional two-person household. Few parents-to-be are quite prepared for the degree of upset that is involved. Having entertained romantic notions of producing a cute and placid infant, they are thrust abruptly into the reality of 3 A.M. feedings, soiled diapers, and apparently inexplicable fits of crying.

Fatigue and anxiety

For virtually all new parents but especially mothers, the physical toll is felt first. It is the mother who literally bears the burden during pregnancy and then undergoes the stress of the birth. In most households, the mother becomes the principal caregiver and yet still carries on her role as homemaker and spouse. It is no wonder that most new mothers report being chronically fatigued.

With physical exhaustion often comes the turmoil of emotional stress, for the father as well as the mother. New parents can be overwhelmed by their sense of responsibility for the infant's well-being; few mothers and fathers get by the first weeks without doubting, at least occasionally, their ability to do the job properly. Mothers who have given up intellectually stimulating or well-paying jobs outside the home to care for the child may resent the sudden interruption of their careers. They may also resent, consciously or unconsciously, being financially dependent on their husbands. Some mothers respond to these pressures by sinking into a brief period of depression—which can be deepened by the hormonal changes that occur in a woman's body after she gives birth.

The myth and reality of motherhood are two different things, as this new mother has found out. Women who experience the greatest difficulties are generally those whose idealized image of mothering clashes at times with the role they actually have to play.

Many traditional fathers find themselves assailed not only by the same uncertainties as their wives, but also by increased financial concerns. Babies mean additional expenses: for cribs, changing tables, diapers, infant clothing, baby-sitters, and sometimes larger housing. The burden of supporting the new family may be compounded by the lost paycheck of the spouse who stays home to care for the infant.

In these and other ways, parenthood can profoundly affect the tenor of a young marriage. The impact can be negative, intensifying marital problems that already existed while simultaneously creating new ones. Time for oneself, for instance, suddenly seems to have become a rare commodity. Because of the baby's demands for attention, periods of quiet intimacy grow scarcer and briefer. Feelings akin to jealousy can also cause friction as the infant temporarily replaces the partner as the focus of attention.

Many marriages, on the other hand, become warmer and far more satisfying after the arrival of a child. A new cooperative spirit can unite a husband and wife as never before. Quiet periods together, because they are rarer, become more valuable and enjoyable. Sex can also take on a deeper meaning. The shared experience of creating and raising a child adds another dimension to life itself.

The inevitable stresses and strains of parenthood can be less upsetting under certain circumstances. For example, the adjustment will be easier when the child is conceived during marriage by a couple that not only is committed to staying together, but also has consciously chosen parenthood. The age of the parents and the length of the marriage when the decision is made can play a surprisingly important role, suggesting that waiting to have children may be a good idea. Studies indicate that older parents are both more attentive to the needs of their children and more satisfied with their lives than first-time parents who are still in their early twenties.

No one can ever predict the temperament or healthiness of a newborn. Some infants seem to be born fretful while others are generally sunny. But even the easygoing baby requires extensive care, and the time parents must devote to their infants can take them by surprise.

There are several steps new parents can take that will make baby care seem less arduous. First of all, expectant mothers and fathers can prepare for parenthood during pregnancy by attending childbirth classes. Such training seems not only to make the birth itself less difficult and more rewarding, but also to help parents build a pleasant sense of anticipation about their new roles. Once the baby arrives, the parents can share the responsibility for attending to the child's needs. Many new fathers are hesitant to handle such small and seemingly delicate beings and may need gentle prodding before they will share in the work and joy of caring for their infant.

However overwhelming her responsibilities may be, a new mother should make an effort to carve out some free time for herself every day as well as setting aside periods when she can talk quietly with her husband. Husband and wife should find ways to make it possible for them to get out of the house without the baby as often as they can. Most important of all, they should find time to quietly discuss the task they are engaged in, particularly as to how they can adjust their expectations to the everyday realities of bringing up a child.

Reaping the rewards

For most mothers and fathers, the rewards of parenthood far outweigh the debits. Many report an enhanced sense of maturity and self-esteem. They often talk of the newborn as the previously missing link that ultimately strengthens their relationship. Most powerful of the rewards, and the most difficult to describe, are the ineffable feelings of love that bind mothers and fathers to their infant.

Bonding, the process by which parents become deeply committed to their young, cannot be rushed or forced. (A related process, attachment, refers to the flow of feeling from child to parent). It may appear with dramatic suddenness in a rush of emotion the first time the parent sees or holds the newborn. More often it develops gradually over a period of weeks or even months as the parent kisses and cuddles the infant while attending to his needs. However it happens, the commitment is so powerful that parents find they are able to endure the sacrifices that are necessary to launch a child into the world.

How you bond to your baby depends on a number of factors. Because the mother has carried the baby in her womb and has given birth to him—and may be breast-feeding him as well—she tends to bond more quickly than the father with the child.

A timetable for bonding?

Exactly when bonding occurs has been the subject of several studies. One theory holds that hormonal changes may make new mothers especially receptive during the first days of an

infant's life. Such claims have had the happy effect of humanizing the maternity wards in many hospitals, which now allow mothers extended periods with their babies, instead of segregating the children in nurseries.

It is a fortunate thing that parent-child bonding is not confined to a single magical moment. Otherwise a parent's relationship with a little one might suffer irreparably should the mother and infant have to be separated during the days and weeks following birth when one or the other of them became ill. Similarly, the already difficult task of adopting a child would prove even more daunting if bonding were dependent upon some particular sensitive period. Without the experience of bonding, adoptive parents would miss much of the thrill that accompanies the moment of bringing a baby home and the whole process of becoming a family.

The ever-growing ties Fortunately for everyone involved, the speed with which bonding occurs does not affect its long-term quality. Once achieved, the parent-child bond deepens as the youngster grows and changes. It is closely tied to the pride and wonder parents experience when they discover that their heir is able to take those first few wobbly steps or has learned to tie his own laces or can balance on a two-wheeler. The joy and excitement only increase as the child grows and begins responding to life in unique and surprising ways. ❖

A father and his son exchange delighted smiles. Such small moments, repeated over time, promote bonding, the process by which the parent develops a deep and abiding love for the child.

Securing Your Loved Ones' Future

First-time parents face the necessity not only of caring for their newborn but also of taking into account his future economic and emotional well-being. Part of this entails financial planning and saving, including adequate insurance protection. In addition, safeguarding the child's future means making legal provisions for his security by drawing up a last will and testament and choosing a legal guardian.

The Right Insurance

In order to pay for the delivery and hospital costs, one form of insurance—medical—ought to be in place before the child is even conceived. If both spouses have group health insurance at work, they should compare the policies before the wife becomes pregnant. Choose the one that provides the better coverage. But if the employers pay all of the premiums for both policies, keep both in effect. Although you cannot collect twice for the same medical expenditure, one policy may supplement the other.

Both parents need life insurance—and a lot of it. Financial planners recommend that each carry policies that will replace 75 to 80 percent of their income in the event of death. Assuming a 7 percent after-tax yield on investment, someone with take-home pay of $25,000 would need a $268,000 policy. Even though some homemakers do not earn an income, they should also be covered. One easy method of determining how much insurance would be adequate involves computing the additional annual cost of hiring child care and then multipying that amount by the number of years that care will be required. If, for example, you have a five-year-old who will need care for ten years and the monthly cost is $1,000, or $12,000 per year, you should purchase a $120,000 policy.

Most financial experts strongly recommend against insuring the life of the youngster. Enormous as the loss of the child would be, it would be a personal tragedy, they point out, not a financial one. They also advise against buying a whole-life policy—one with a stated cash-in value at a given age—for the child to help pay for her college. This investment seldom proves to be as profitable as others.

Parents frequently overlook another kind of insurance: disability coverage, which provides income if an illness or accident prevents a worker from resuming job or career.

According to one survey, only about one-fourth of American workers have long-term disability insurance. This is true despite the fact that, until sixty-five, disability is far more likely to occur than death. The risk of a thirty-five-year-old man's becoming disabled is three times greater than his risk of dying during the same period. Coverage that will replace about 60 percent of pretax income is recommended. If you have other funds available to back you up, you can save considerably on premiums by buying a policy that delays the payment of disability income for six months.

Saving For College

Research indicates that the cost of higher education is rising faster than consumer prices. Estimates of the cost of four years of schooling at a public university beginning in the year 2000 range as high as $45,000. At a highly rated private college the cost might even exceed $130,000. Obviously, not everyone will be able to create a nest egg that large. Amassing $130,000 would require the investment of $3,800 every year after the child's birth at a 7 percent after-tax yield. But professionals are unanimous in their advice that the important thing is to start saving now, no matter how modest the amount.

They recommend a diversified savings plan. The plan might range in risk and payoff from low-yielding government-insured certificates of deposit to potentially more profitable investments in the stock market—in mutual funds and individual blue-chip stocks. You may also want to buy a zero-coupon municipal bond, which is tax-free and has the advantage of providing a safe, guaranteed rate of return. During its lifetime, it pays no interest to you, but at maturity you get the principal, plus the compounded interest. Thus a 7 percent zero-coupon bond purchased for $10,000 would guarantee you $27,590 in fifteen years.

Another useful savings device is to establish a custodial account for your children. Federal tax laws permit each parent to transfer up to $10,000 a year into each child's account tax-free. But there are drawbacks. For children younger than fourteen, annual earnings above $1,000 are taxed at the parents' higher rate, not at the child's own lower rate. Also, the money you transfer into the account is no longer yours. When the child reaches the age of

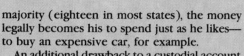

majority (eighteen in most states), the money legally becomes his to spend just as he likes—to buy an expensive car, for example.

An additional drawback to a custodial account is that it may eventually affect your child's eligibility for financial aid. Most colleges and universities offer various scholarships, grants, workstudy programs and low-interest loans to supplement the funds of many middle-income families. Some schools, in calculating eligibility, give greater weight to the child's assets than to the parents' on the grounds that the child can afford to part with a larger portion of savings because he has fewer financial obligations.

A few schools offer an alternative to systematic saving for education. Parents of even an infant can prepay four years of tuition in one lump sum at a price sharply discounted from the projected costs when the child enters college. The problem with these "tuition futures" is that if the child should decide not to enroll at that particular school or should fail to win admission, only the original investment will be refunded—without interest.

Writing a Will

Every parent needs a will. More than two-thirds of all adults die without one—intestate, in legal jargon. They thus abdicate to the laws of their state all decisions relating to the distribution of their property and the rearing of their minor children. Those who die intestate also risk penalizing their heirs with large estate taxes and costs that accompany the government's intrusion into such matters.

You can write a simple will yourself or hire a lawyer to do it—for a reasonable fee. Several states even provide rudimentary do-it-yourself wills. These so-called no-frills wills consist of standard forms; you simply fill in the blanks, check the appropriate boxes, and sign your name—in front of witnesses in some states. If you write your own will or use the do-it-yourself form, it makes sense to ask a lawyer familiar with your state's tax and testamentary laws to review it for a small fee.

However you draw it up, your will ought to contain two key provisions in addition to naming your heirs. It should appoint the executor who, under the jurisdiction of the court, takes charge of supervising the settlement of your estate by inventorying all property, paying debts and taxes, and distributing the assets according to your wishes. It should also name the legal guardian who will look after your orphaned children until they come of age.

Choosing a guardian is probably the biggest challenge in drawing up a will, for the guardian will be managing your most precious legacies—your children—in the scary, but unlikely, event that both you and your spouse should die. You will probably want to select a relative, perhaps a sister or brother, or a close friend. In making the choice, take into account such factors as the potential guardian's age, health, financial circumstances, marital stability, and the compatibility of his or her children with yours. Most of all, you should feel comfortable with the candidate's cultural and religious values: Will he or she raise your children much as you would? Talk it over with the person before making the commitment and select a backup in case your prime selection is unable to serve.

Lawyers often recommend establishing a trust agreement in connection with the will. By putting your estate into a so-called testamentary trust that takes effect after your death, you can dictate how the money will be spent for your children's benefit. In some circumstances, such an arrangement can provide substantial tax savings for the estate. You select the trustee, who may also be the legal guardian or perhaps someone with more financial expertise. The trustee will be free to write the necessary checks without having to post an expensive bond or getting tangled up in judicial red tape.

Once you have made your will, review it periodically in the light of changing circumstances. You can change it anytime by adding a codicil—a written amendment—or by revoking it and writing an entirely new one.

45

How Many Is Right for You?

Even as a husband and wife are making the transition to parenthood with all its tribulations and rewards, they face a momentous decision: whether or not to have another child. If they opt for a second offspring, they must then make up their minds how soon to have it. Or perhaps they decide to have several more. If so, they must give thought to how they want the children spaced (*pages 50–53*).

Such choices were virtually unheard of until recent decades. Before the development of modern methods of birth control, the number and spacing of children was largely a matter of chance. However, parents today—whether they use birth control measures or the rhythm method—can determine the size of their family.

Large family vs. small
Throughout most of human history, large families have been regarded as the norm. Children were once considered economic assets, providing the manual labor to work the land and supporting their parents through old age. It was regarded as essential to produce more offspring than actually needed because so many of them were expected to succumb to disease.

In the more developed countries, economic necessity is no longer a main reason for having large families. Even the definition of "large" has undergone change. Less than a century ago, families of seven or eight children were commonplace; in today's world, a family with four children is considered a large one.

Experts cite several advantages inherent in the family of four or more offspring. Children with several brothers and sisters become socialized much more rapidly than youngsters who are only children, learning to share, to show consideration for others, and to develop self-control. Large families can also engender a climate of emotional security where not just the parents but siblings provide ready-made companions and sources of strength—everyday playmates and mentors as well as protectors, confidants, and counselors in times of stress.

But there can be disadvantages to being part of a large family. Many parents lack the money required today to feed, clothe, and house more than a couple of children. And when both parents must work to support a large family, they may lack the time and energy to devote the love and attention their children need. Even intellect may be affected. Surveys indicate that intelligence-test scores tend to decline as family size increases. This intellectual "dilution," as it has been called, seems to come about when each succeeding youngster finds himself having less opportunity for contact with the parents.

Smaller families, by contrast, appear to suffer less from intellectual dilution—as well as from stretched-thin supplies of money. If there are fewer siblings around to create a large, warm family circle, each child is compensated by having more opportunity for quiet, enriching times he can share with the grown-ups.

Recipient of the most parental attention, of course, is the only child. The one-child family was long viewed with pity and disdain. According to the stereotype, the child inevitably was not only spoiled, but as an American psychologist expressed it less than a century ago, also "jealous, selfish, egotistical, dependent, aggressive, domineering, quarrelsome." Today, general opinion is so negative that the most widely cited reason that parents give for producing a second offspring is to prevent the first one from growing up an only child.

Nonetheless, more and more American parents are

Brothers and sisters in the large family at left play an impromptu game of ring-around-a-rosy with their parents. Studies have shown that children who grow up with many siblings learn quickly to share, and that they develop self-control and consideration for others. Only children, like the little boy above, are often reluctant to make friends and may need an extra push from their parents to help them relate to their peers.

stopping at one. Many factors underlie this trend, from high divorce rates and concerns about world overpopulation to two-career marriages and the tendency to delay the birth of the first child until an age when increasing probability of infertility or danger of birth defects may make having a second one unwise. The burgeoning cost of raising a child and an emphasis on the needs of parents as well as the children's also play a role.

Not the least of the reasons for the increase in one-child families is evidence that tells parents it is all right—maybe even better—to have only one. Recent studies have demolished most of the old notions about only children. The results point to few negative effects and many positive ones. Perhaps because of greater parental attention and expectations, only children are generally better students and higher achievers than children from larger families. Considering that they have always formed a small minority in any era, surprising numbers of only children appear in *Who's Who* and on other lists of prominent scholars, artists, and leaders. And though they seem less sociable than children from larger families, only children rank just as high on measures of self-esteem and happiness.

Many parents of only children also appear to benefit. In one survey, for example, women with one child were more likely to report they were happy with their lives than either childless women or mothers of two or more children.

For all of the new enthusiasm about only children, experts are quick to name some built-in shortcomings. For example, parents risk losing all if the only child should die. And only children face the prospect of someday caring for their aged mothers and fathers without the help of siblings.

Parents also run the risk of smothering an only child with attention, distorting his view of himself and his place in the world. Sometimes parents become excessively protective, while their children grow tentative and become shy or withdrawn. Similarly, parents should not push an only child too hard to achieve. Unreasonably high expectations can lead to disappointment, frustration, and distress.

A father and daughter enjoy the thrill of a slide ride together. A child's delight in simple pleasures is infectious; sharing them, say many parents, is one of parenting's greatest joys.

Can You Determine Your Child's Sex?

"A boy for you, a girl for me." The words of the old song hint at one of the enduring dreams of parenthood: to be able to choose the gender of your child. People have been coming up with methods to try to help them do just that since ancient times. Aristotle's formula was to make love in the north wind to conceive a boy, in the south wind for a girl. His Greek countryman and the father of medicine, Hippocrates, recognized far ahead of his time that the male sperm determines the gender of the offspring; he advised tying a string around the right testicle to trigger the production of male-bearing seed and around the left one if a female offspring was wanted.

Scientists today are still trying to find ways to make sex selection possible. The goal is to enhance the chances of fertilizing the woman's ovum with sperm bearing the desired sex-determining chromosome. A sperm cell with an X chromosome results in female offspring; a sperm with a Y produces male children (*pages 20–21*). Both X-bearing and Y-bearing sperm are produced in approximately equal quantities, giving the lie to the commonly held notion that boys can run in one family, while girls run in another.

One sex-selection technique popular during the 1970s depended upon the frequency of intercourse and the supposed influence of the acid-alkaline balance in the vagina upon the two types of sperm. Now generally discredited, this method advocated douching before sexual relations with a vinegar solution to give the advantage to the X-bearing, female-producing sperm, or with a baking soda solution to favor those sperm carrying the male-producing Y chromosome.

In the meantime, several scientists have focused on the timing of conception and the lifespans of the two kinds of sperm as the key to sex selection. Because the Y-bearing (male) sperm has a longer survival rate than the X-bearing variety, some of the researchers say that intercourse occurring several days before ovulation increases the odds of a male child. But others put the optimum period for producing boys nearer to the actual time of ovulation. The problem is that the specialists have drawn contradictory conclusions, in part because in some of the experiments insemination was carried out artificially, with the sperm being injected into the female, while in the others intercourse was allowed to occur naturally.

More recent experiments have involved laboratory separation of a sample of the husband's sperm into the two types. One depends on the differing speeds of the X and Y sperm. Another separates the sperm by weight, the X-bearing sperm being heavier than the Y. Still another relies on the fact that the two types carry different electrical charges. With all three methods, once the desired type—X or Y—is separated, it can then be used to artificially inseminate the prospective mother. Although these methods may be long on ingenuity, none, in fact, has been proven successful in practice—and all have stirred controversy.

Critics fear that parents able to choose their child's gender would drastically tip the boy-girl birth balance in favor of males. (The ratio at birth is now 105 males to every 100 females.) They point to the fact that many societies place a higher value on boys than on girls. A survey of Americans found that among childless women with a preference, more than two-thirds wanted a boy as their first child.

But sex selection could prove to be literally a lifesaver for families with a history of sex-linked hereditary diseases. Genetic disorders such as hemophilia and certain types of muscular dystrophy primarily affect males. The female carriers of the defective genes could choose to conceive only girls, thus sparing the males a lifetime of suffering.

To enlarge the world of an only child, parents should make sure he has playmates. Nursery schools are places where only children can meet peers and engage in the give-and-take—friction as well as friendship—that characterizes sibling relationships. Parents of only children would also do well to foster close ties with relatives. Only children can miss the ready companionship a sibling would provide. Getting to know aunts and uncles and cousins can assuage this isolation.

Making the decision One, two, or three? How many children are right for you may depend upon practical concerns: income, careers, the stability of your marriage. You will remember what persuaded you to have the first child. You may want to provide a companion for him or try for a child of the opposite sex.

For many parents, their own childhood experiences are decisive. Those who had close relationships with a number of siblings often want to recreate a similar situation; parents who were only children are apt to want fewer offspring. ⋰

Spacing for the Good of All

How far apart your children are spaced can have dramatic impact on the life of the family. The length of the intervals between births can not only affect sibling behavior and your relationships with each child, but even strengthen or undermine your marriage. The impact, however, varies from family to family, depending upon matters as diverse as your financial situation and your youngsters' personalities.

Most American parents are choosing to increase the

One-Year Gap

Two-Year Gap

interval between their children's birth. The interval currently averages two years and eight months, the widest it has been since World War II. This longer wait, like the decrease in family size, largely reflects the increased reliability of birth control methods—and the awareness that too many children too soon can generate unneeded stress.

Just as researchers have learned that there is no ideal family size, they also have found that no ideal spacing exists. Various intervals have advantages and disadvantages; the pros and cons of five different intervals are discussed below and on the following pages.

When it comes to spacing, many family-planning experts urge parents to choose what is best for them rather than what they think is good for the children. In their view, the spacing that is right for parents will end up benefiting the entire family, so long as it can be done realistically.

Advantages

Closeness in age ensures that the children will have common interests and will be live-in playmates for each other; a small gap also tends to foster emotional closeness between the siblings.

Parents who have two or more children in close succession can limit all the diapering and other tedious and demanding tasks of infant care to one relatively brief period in their lives. Such clustering also enables the mother to return to her career, if she has one, sooner. Short intervals between children may also be advantageous to mothers older than thirty-five who are concerned about declining fertility or the greater risk of birth defects occurring with advancing age.

Disadvantages

Many child-development experts advise against a one-year gap. One-year-olds often become clingy and miserable with the birth of a sibling, turning jealous and competitive seven to ten months later, when the rival starts to crawl. Parents may only worsen the situation by pushing the toddler to act more grown-up or by treating the two children as if both were infants.

For parents, too, one-year spacing can bring huge emotional and physical demands—the pregnancies, the interrupted sleep, two very dependent children, the loss of time alone together. Such spacing can deprive parents of the energy they must have to meet their young ones' needs.

With a two-year gap, the two-year-old is ready for group play with her age-mates. Whenever possible, parents should arrange for the toddler to join a play group, thus giving themselves a little more time to be alone with the baby. Later, as the growing siblings become companions with many shared interests, the parents can plan activities that both will enjoy.

While rivalry and competition are heightened between children who have only two years separating them, the gap allows the younger child to imitate and learn from the older. Admiration can lead to a strong friendship that can endure into adulthood.

Two is a difficult age for both child and parents, particularly as the toddler struggles to individualize herself. A new baby at this critical time may compound her problems, especially since she lacks the cognitive and language skills to recognize and verbalize her needs and feelings. To get attention, she may cry often or behave in an aggressive manner toward the baby.

The conflicted parents may find their time and emotions seriously strained. At times they may be too occupied with the baby to tend to the toddler's emotional needs, thus causing her to repeat her demands—and state them more forcefully.

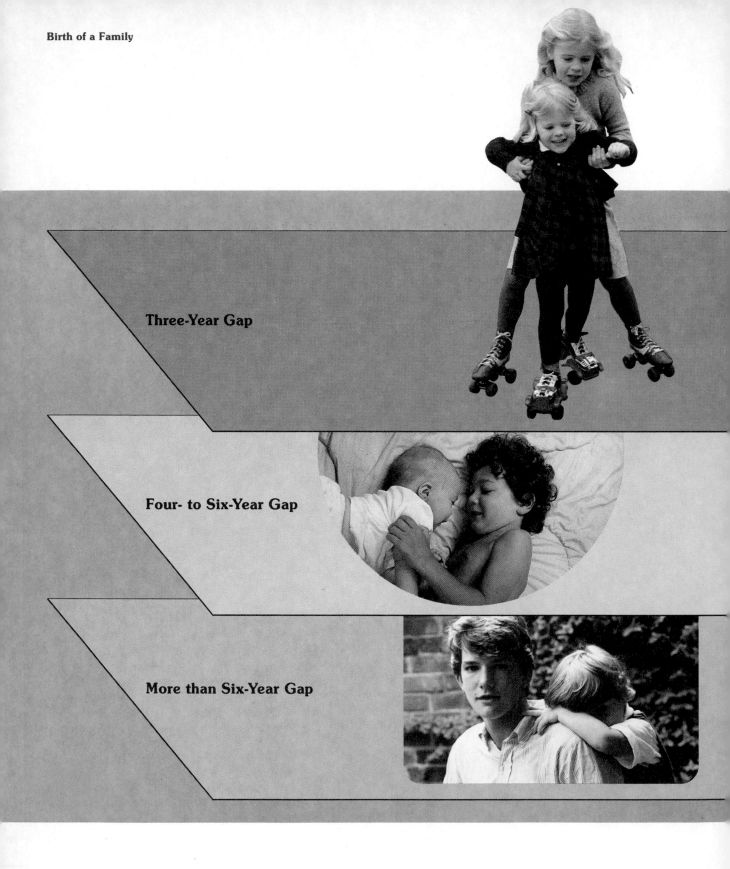

Three-Year Gap

Four- to Six-Year Gap

More than Six-Year Gap

Advantages

More self-sufficient and self-assured, the three-year-old probably can dress herself and may be attending nursery school. She is able to understand that sometimes other people's needs compete with hers and can better tolerate delays and frustrations. She will also have begun to model herself after her parents; in watching them take care of the baby, she may turn to her doll and imitate their behavior. Often she can be helpful and cooperative.

Thanks to the three-year gap, many parents feel they have had a good breather. Furthermore, their three-year-old's growing autonomy affords them more time to care for the newcomer.

Mentally and physically, the older sibling is ready to join in the care of the newborn, perhaps helping feed or amuse the baby, or taking on such chores as sorting the laundry. He can control some of his jealous, aggressive impulses. As the two grow older, they can play together, and this will help develop social skills in the second-born. The baby admires and learns from his big brother, who takes great pride in the little one's achievements. Many parents say that the children's good relationship reduces considerably the stress they might otherwise experience caring for two.

When as much as six years separate them, the older child may adopt an almost parental role toward his sibling. He can help tutor and protect him while learning valuable lessons in nurturing.

Parents of such widely spaced children are able to give their first child their full attention during his formative years. When the new baby arrives, they are older and perhaps more mature, relaxed and skillful as parents. They may have an easier time financially and can plan effectively for the children's college educations with tuition costs spread out over a longer period.

Disadvantages

Some researchers find sibling rivalry to be most intense between children who are spaced two to four years apart. Three-year-olds can become especially difficult and demanding with the arrival of the new baby. Studies, however, indicate that much depends upon the parents. Because sibling rivalry often involves a competition for parental attention, parents can reduce the jealousy and squabbling by striving to provide more or less equal attention to both youngsters. By virtue of her age, the older child is capable of talking about her jealous feelings, instead of acting them out against the baby.

Despite the wide gap in age and maturity, the older child may be hostile to the new sibling. As the only child for a number of years, he has enjoyed undivided attention; needing to share his parents' affection may be hard for him. He may fantasize that his parents had another child because they found something wrong with him. If the older one is just starting school, he may feel that the younger one has replaced him at home and hold this against the baby.

Also, the children's divergent ages and interests make it difficult for parents to plan activities both siblings can enjoy.

This wide age gap can produce children with very little in common and no reason or basis for developing bonds of affection. The older child may even resent the second's arrival and balk at giving up any part of the parents' attention that has been his for so long.

Parents may find it hard to adapt again to the needs of an infant. They may also find it difficult to juggle their children's widely different interests and schedules.

Sibling Bonds

The birth of your second child begins a new and very different phase in the life of your family. Gone are the comparatively simple days of nurturing a single child. Now you must forge through the labor-intensive first years with a demanding new baby, all the while meeting the needs of your firstborn and convincing her that there is room in your world for both of them. Although ultimately rewarding, this is invariably a juggling act that is sure to call upon all your reserves of patience and understanding.

For the firstborn child, the transition from only child to older sibling is understandably difficult. Accustomed to life as the star attraction, she suddenly finds herself competing for your attention and perhaps doubting your love. She must learn all at once that few things in life are exclusively hers—not Mommy, not Daddy, not even the crib that once was hers. And to make matters worse, she is reaching an age when she is expected to begin to assume responsibilities, whereas her rival has no obligations other than eating and sleeping. The newborn, in the meantime, will gradually come to know that while youth has its privileges, it also has its price in the form of a sometimes domineering or critical older sibling. The stage is thus set for the child-size power struggles that can get out of hand if insensitively handled by the parents.

But rivalry between siblings is only part of the story. Even more important is sibling loyalty. As seen in the love of the two sisters at right, the distinctive closeness that many siblings share forms the basis for what can be a rewarding and supportive lifelong connection.

In this section, you will see how you can keep rivalry from getting out of hand and at the same time encourage good relationships.

A Uniquely Complex Relationship

The special magic of blowing soap bubbles captivates a brother and sister. As daily companions, siblings gain what psychoanalyst Erik Erikson has called the "irreplaceable experience of a shared childhood."

Despite the current trend toward smaller families, relatively few children grow up without the company of at least one sibling. In fact, far from diluting the sibling relationship, the shrinking size of the American family is at least partly responsible for a growing dependence of siblings on one another. The high incidence of divorce and the dramatic increase in the number of working mothers also heighten this interdependence.

The experience of sharing childhood with a sibling has a profound effect on development. Subtly and not so subtly, it shapes each sibling's personality, intelligence, and self-image. These changes begin with the arrival of the second child, when the firstborn son or daughter undergoes what amounts to a dethroning.

Begrudgingly leaving the role of only child, your firstborn may greet the baby's birth with anything from indifference to half-hearted pleasure. More than likely, however, he will be resentful. He may also be angry at you for bringing the little intruder home in the first place and become more demanding or babyish in an effort to win back the love he imagines he has lost. Nearly all children are upset by the birth of a sibling. But given time to adjust, most firstborns gradually accept their new siblings and their new roles as big brothers and sisters. And thus begins the formation of the web of emotions that characterizes a sibling relationship. Love and hate both play a part in this bond, together with envy, competition, empathy, and admiration.

As a consequence, the nature and intensity of sibling relationships vary widely. Some siblings enjoy a warm and affectionate one. Others seem to throw off sparks at every contact. The majority seesaw between these two extremes, playing happily for the most part, then quarreling furiously, only to make up and fight again another day. It is a mistake to think of the quarrelsome behavior as a sign of your failure. To expect your children to live in unruffled harmony is to expect the impossible. Still, some parents wonder why their youngsters fight and bicker. After all, their children have the same parents and live in the same home. So why don't they get along better than they do?

Factors affecting relationships

Until recently, the most frequently cited answers to that question were centered on birth order, age gap, and gender. Certainly, these factors are important in determining the quality of sibling relationships and in shaping the personality of each child. But even more important than these are the influences of each child's temperament—over which parents have little control—and the quality of the individual parent-child relationships.

Just because two children live in close daily contact does not mean that they have to like each other. Even under the best of circumstances, one child's personality may simply clash with another's. Likewise, as much as parents want to believe that they treat each of their children alike, no parent really does. Invariably, oldest children are treated differently from youngest children, sons differently from daughters, toddlers differently from preschoolers. And there is nothing wrong with treating each child differently. Fair, not equal, treatment is the prescription for success in the raising of siblings.

Raising siblings may be a challenge, but it is also a unique opportunity to foster love and respect within a family. Siblings also offer the convenience of a live-in playmate. Unlike only children, siblings are faced with a continual need to practice such social skills as cooperation and negotiation within the home. For younger children, the presence of an older brother or sister also provides a ready role model, a chance to learn from the experience of someone else. Moreover, sibling relationships can lay the groundwork for broader social understanding: teaching children to respect the feelings of others, to share and compete, to forgive and trust. These are necessary lessons, best learned in childhood. ❖

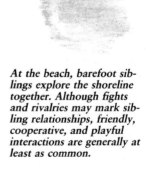

At the beach, barefoot siblings explore the shoreline together. Although fights and rivalries may mark sibling relationships, friendly, cooperative, and playful interactions are generally at least as common.

Mustering her strength, a girl gives an older brother a ride on her tricycle. Play in which roles are reversed can offer a boost to the little one's self-esteem.

Starting Out Right

The impending birth of your second child may be a blessed event to you; but to your firstborn, who sees his crib commandeered for the newcomer and his parents increasingly preoccupied, the event may seem anything but blessed. The new baby will quite predictably be a threat to your first child's security. And while there is nothing you can do or say that will completely spare the little one's feelings, there are steps you can take to make his adjustment easier.

Questions about reproduction   Start at the very beginning, with the announcement of your pregnancy. In telling your firstborn that a baby is on the way, keep his needs and feelings foremost in your mind. For a child younger than two, this may mean delaying the announcement until the final two or three months of pregnancy—eternity enough to any small child. On the other hand, if your toddler notices changes in your appearance or behavior and asks about it, by all means tell him the news. Do not take the chance that he might interpret your expanding abdomen as evidence of some dread disease or fear that the fact that you are napping more frequently indicates declining interest in him.

An older child should get the news early in the pregnancy, preferably as soon as you find out yourself, but certainly before she hears it from a friend or neighbor. Whatever your youngster's age, break the news to her simply and honestly. Be direct but also thoughtful, taking care to refer to the new arrival as "our baby" rather than "Mommy's and Daddy's baby." Avoid making empty promises. For example, do not tell your preschooler that she will soon have a new playmate, since it will be quite a while before the baby can really be a companion. Do not tell her how much she will love her new brother or sister, either. It is quite possible that she will not in the beginning, and being told that she should will only make her feel guilty. Also, never be so bold as to promise a brother or sister, unless you know the unborn baby's sex. To do so only invites disappointment, should your prediction prove false.

Finally, use the occasion of announcing the pregnancy to reassure your child that her place in your heart remains a special one and that even though the baby will demand attention, you will still find the time to do things with her. Tell her of the advantages of being a big sister, but stop short of hurrying her to grow up. Pediatrician T. Berry Brazelton has noted that many parents make that mistake at this stage, in part by giving the firstborn more responsibility. Without really meaning to, they are shoving the youngster out of the nest.

In a moment of closeness, a mother tells her firstborn that a baby is on the way. She will keep her explanation of where babies come from simple but be ready to answer any questions her daughter might ask.

Now more than ever, your child needs to know that the nest is big enough to hold everyone in the family.

The news that the family is expecting a new baby may prompt your older child to start asking you about the origin of babies. The questions he asks can range from the curious to the comical. Your toddler may wonder how and what the baby eats while it is inside Mommy's tummy, where it sleeps, and how it goes to the bathroom. These are all questions of the utmost importance to a small child. An inquisitive older child may also want to know how the baby could get inside Mommy in the first place and how it is going to get out.

Your answers should, of course, be truthful but kept to the child's own level. "Mommy and Daddy made it" may be enough to satisfy a two-year-old. A four-year-old, on the other hand, will almost certainly follow up with additional questions. Tell him only as much as you think he wants to know, rather than explaining the whole reproductive process. If he feels a need for additional information, he will ask. In discussing body parts and functions, it is generally better to use the adult terms rather than searching for metaphors. At the same time, it may be enough to explain only that "Mommies have a special place inside for babies to grow" and "The doctor will help when the baby is ready to come out." Children's books can also be useful when it comes to explaining these matters. For some especially good ones, see the list on page 66.

Do not be alarmed, however, if despite your frankness and honesty, your youngster clings to his own version of events rather than accepting your explanation. Some children simply prefer to preserve their fantasies of where babies come from or to weave their own versions of biological processes into the facts.

Nine months is a long time for prospective parents as well as for prospective siblings. And while every pregnancy has its trying moments, those moments would be all the more trying were it not for your own excitement and sense of anticipation.

Toward that end, give him plenty of opportunities to feel the baby moving inside your tummy, and if your doctor permits it, bring the child along on a prenatal visit so he can listen to the baby's heartbeat. Whenever you are out of the house, keep an eye open for other babies and point out their big brothers and sisters. If your hospital offers sibling preparation classes, by all means enroll your child (*pages 62–65*). And make a prebirth visit to the maternity ward so he will know where you will be when the baby comes.

At home, you can involve your preschooler in getting the nursery ready. You can also invite him to join in prenatal exercises. Some parents find that it helps to buy a lifelike doll with newborn features and encourage the child to take care of it. Later, as the due date nears, let the youngster help with the packing of Mommy's hospital bag—and be sure to include his photograph.

Most important, avoid last-minute upsets in his life. If you are planning any changes in his routine—whether it is moving from crib to bed or weaning him from the bottle—do so well before the newcomer's arrival. If the new baby will be using the firstborn's crib, you can defuse a potentially upsetting situation by disassembling the crib and storing it for several months before the baby is brought home.

Final preparations As the delivery date approaches, it is important to prepare your child for the inevitable separation that occurs when Mommy goes to the hospital to have the baby. Start by making certain that your youngster knows exactly what the plans are and how long the hospital stay is likely to last. Explain where the child will be staying and who will be taking care of her. As a rule, the less change in her routine the better. Accordingly, if it is at all possible, have her remain at home with a relative, a friend, or her usual babysitter. And make sure, when you are leaving for the hospital, that you say good-bye and discuss when you are going to return.

Some expectant mothers record a few bedtime stories for their children to listen to during the separation, embellishing each with a loving message and a warm goodnight kiss. Other parents find it helpful to put a picture of her mother in the child's bedroom and to give her some special responsibility, such as taking care of an inexpensive piece of jewelry.

Siblings in the delivery room

Some parents nowadays want their older children to have firsthand experience of the birth of siblings and thus arrange for their presence at labor and delivery. Although this practice is not widespread with preschoolers, it is an option at more and more hospitals when the doctors themselves approve. Proponents contend that the older child's presence at the birth will strengthen the bond with the new sibling and reduce rivalry later. Detractors, on the other hand, argue that the experience is too traumatic for young children and that their presence can be a major distraction during the birth process.

Make age and temperament the primary considerations in the decision of whether you want to include your child in your birth plans. Some youngsters may indeed find the experience frightening or confusing—or at the very least, boring. Keep in mind, too, that a child should never be forced to attend the birth, especially if she has already said that she has no interest in being there.

If your youngster will be present, be sure she has been briefed in advance—perhaps through a children's birth-preparation class or a visit to your pediatrician. You do not want her to be surprised by the pain of strong contractions, bleeding, common surgical procedures like episiotomies, the blue color of the newborn, the cutting of the umbilical cord, or the appearance of the placenta. If the father will be coaching during labor, have a friend or relative present to attend to the child's needs and questions. And be sure to let your youngster know that she may leave the delivery room at any time she wishes and need not return.

When the baby arrives

Even a well-prepared child is bound to be upset to one degree or another by the birth of a sibling. Begin immediately to soothe any bruised feelings by telephoning as soon after the birth as is practical. Invite the youngster to visit you at the hospital and to meet the new baby. When he does, make sure that the visit is limited to the immediate family and give him as much time and attention as you can. Tell him how much you miss him and ask about his activities. Let him set the pace for his introduction to the newcomer. If he is old enough, ask him if he would like to hold the baby while seated in a chair.

When it is time for your firstborn to go home, expect some tears and perhaps even a tantrum. After all, having just found you, he is not eager to lose you again. Do not worry that the scene might bother the hospital staff—they will have encountered such problems before.

Learning How to Be a Big Sister or Brother

Becoming a sibling can have its ups and downs. To ease the process, some hospitals offer classes that prepare "expectant" big brothers and sisters for the arrival of the new baby. These generally include a tour of the maternity ward and nursery, a simple explanation of a newborn's capabilities, and a frank discussion of the mixed feelings that children can expect to experience when the baby comes. Finally, the youngsters are given some practical training in baby care, more to make them aware of their parents' responsibilities than to turn them into trusty aides.

Helping the older child to accept the new family member is perhaps the program's greatest benefit. For some little ones, a few of the finer details may go unabsorbed, but a sense of anticipation is stimulated. After completing one sibling-preparation class, an excited three-year-old asked her mother: "Are we going to get the baby from the hospital today?"

A nurse explains to a family the topics she will cover in the hour-long preparedness class. The father holds a book about babies his son can take home.

Siblings-to-be peek into the nursery. So that they can see what a day-old infant looks like, the nurse at right has wheeled one up to the window.

The nurse gives the children a closer look at the newborn, pointing to the place where the umbilical cord was attached.

With a doll as model, the nurse explains how the baby receives nourishment and oxygen through the umbilical cord. Here the cord is a twisted stocking, the uterus a knitted bag.

Seated on the classroom floor, the nurse holds up a chart showing developmental stages during the course of pregnancy.

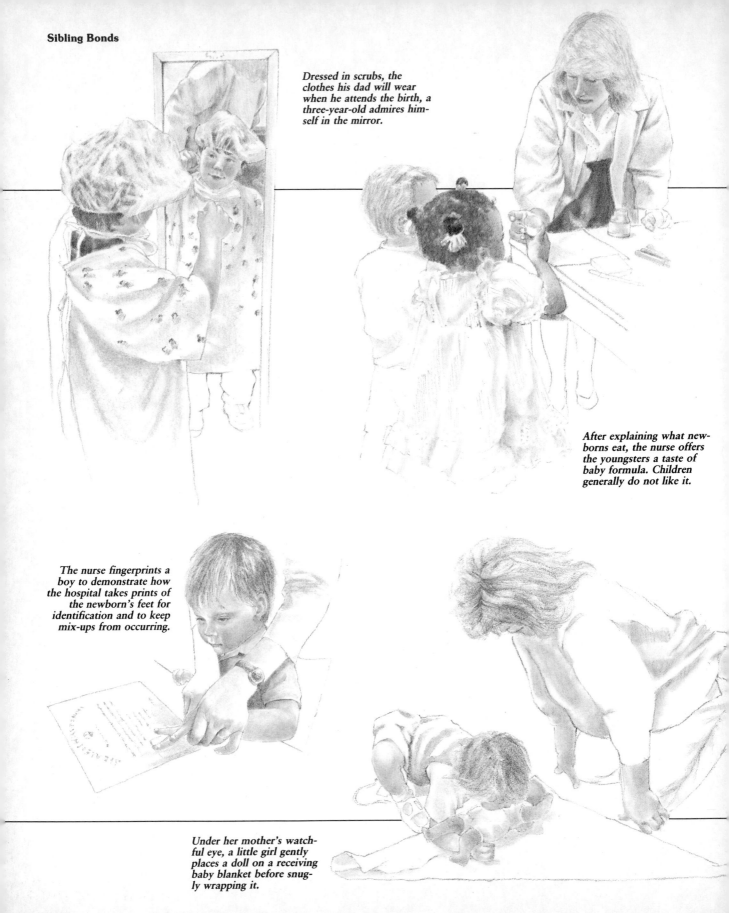

Dressed in scrubs, the clothes his dad will wear when he attends the birth, a three-year-old admires himself in the mirror.

After explaining what newborns eat, the nurse offers the youngsters a taste of baby formula. Children generally do not like it.

The nurse fingerprints a boy to demonstrate how the hospital takes prints of the newborn's feet for identification and to keep mix-ups from occurring.

Under her mother's watchful eye, a little girl gently places a doll on a receiving baby blanket before snugly wrapping it.

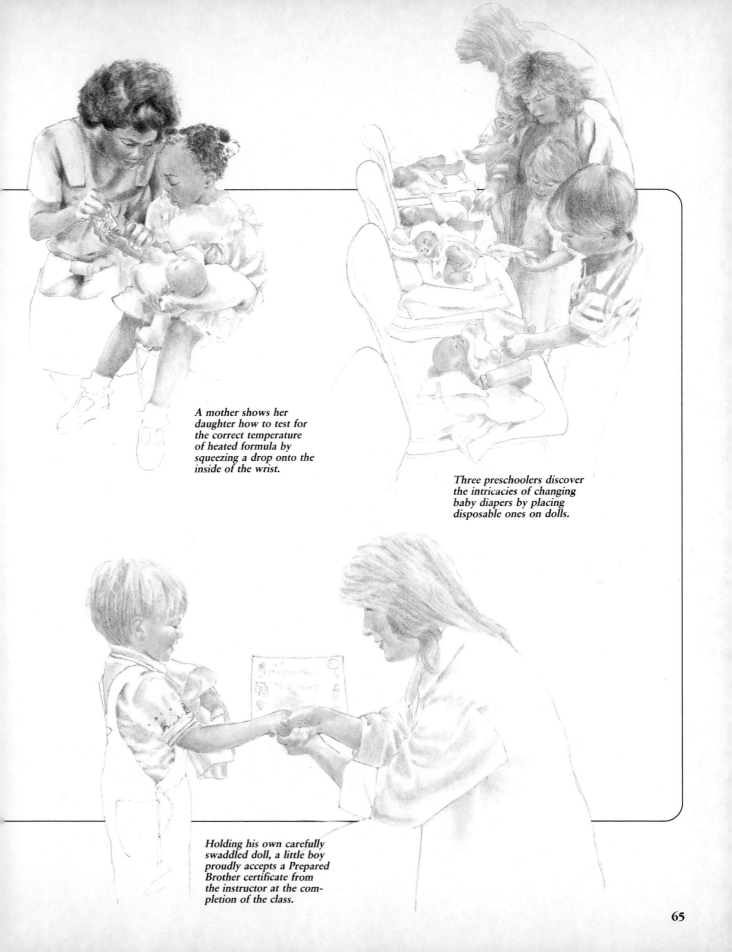

A mother shows her daughter how to test for the correct temperature of heated formula by squeezing a drop onto the inside of the wrist.

Three preschoolers discover the intricacies of changing baby diapers by placing disposable ones on dolls.

Holding his own carefully swaddled doll, a little boy proudly accepts a Prepared Brother certificate from the instructor at the completion of the class.

During the rest of your hospital stay, telephone him frequently between his visits. Dad can also serve as courier, carrying home an occasional note, a bouquet of flowers, or a small gift scavenged from your hospital tray, such as a packet of jelly or a container of juice. If you have an instant camera or can borrow one, you may wish to have yourself photographed with and without the baby and send the pictures along as a special present from you and the baby.

Special circumstances An ill or premature baby presents special problems for the family, all the more so if the setback delays the mother's return from the hospital. The firstborn may be eager to see the long-awaited new baby. If this is the case, she should be encouraged to be patient and—when the infant's condition permits—be allowed to see the little brother or sister. Do not hide the situation from your older child, however, whether it is illness, prematurity, or even the possibility of death. Explain matters in terms the youngster can understand. Since some children develop feelings of guilt in these circumstances, reassure your youngster that the baby's troubles are nobody's fault. If your own hospital stay is extended, have the child visit you as often as possible and be mindful to shower her with plenty of love during this trying time.

Should the baby die, answer your child's questions honestly. Do not appear to ignore the death by concealing grief. If she is old enough, encourage the youngster to talk about the baby, to join in the mourning and, if you wish, to attend the funeral. Blessedly, the chances of a child dying are not great.

Coming home The happy event of bringing a healthy baby home from the hospital is a special moment in all parents' lives. But this is a time to be particularly aware of the needs and feelings of your older child. In fact, in order to be able to devote extra attention to your firstborn, declare this a family day and ask friends and relatives to please postpone their visits until later.

If possible, let your firstborn come along on the trip to and from the hospital. Should it be necessary for the youngster to remain behind at some place other than your house or apartment, arrange to have him brought home after you have arrived and the baby is settled. Alternatively, should your older child be there waiting, it is a good idea for Mother to enter first to greet him while Dad trails behind with the infant. When friends and relatives do come by to see the baby, quietly remind them to give your older child a little attention; often in their

Books about Birth and Babies

- Alexander, Martha. *Nobody Asked Me If I Wanted a Baby Sister.* Ages 2+.

- Andry, Andrew C., and Steven Schepp. *How Babies Are Made.* Ages 2+.

- Berger, Terry. *A New Baby.* Ages 3+.

- Cole, Joanna. *The New Baby at Your House.* Ages 5+.

- Holland, Viki. *We Are Having a Baby.* Ages 2+.

- Mayle, Peter. *"Where Did I Come From?"* Ages 5+.

- Rankin, Chrissy. *How Life Begins.* Ages 5+.

- Sheffield, Margaret. *Where Do Babies Come From?* Ages 5+.

- Stein, Sara Bonnett. *Making Babies.* Ages 2+.

excitement, they forget to do so.

During all the weeks ahead, continue to be solicitous of the older child's needs and feelings, taking care to minimize changes in his daily routine and to avoid drastic cutbacks in the amount of time and attention he receives. Encourage him to take an interest in the baby. Talk about the infant as a person with needs, wants, likes, and dislikes. And draw attention to the baby's interest in the older child with such comments as, "See, she's looking at you," or "She likes it when you hold her hand." By the same token, avoid saying things like "Tell me later," or "Can't you see that I'm busy?" Such remarks may only reinforce the older child's feelings of neglect or rejection. You might also encourage him to help you care for the baby, then look for opportunities to praise him for his assistance. All this, of course, cannot come at the expense of your new baby, who requires a considerable amount of care and attention herself. The older sibling must be taught to understand that the baby needs Mommy and Daddy, too.

When firstborn meets newborn, as here, their relationship is already compelling to the older child. Many firstborns become intensely interested in the infant and make up games in which they are baby or parent.

First reactions No amount of sensitive handling on your part will guarantee that your older child will greet her new sibling with undiluted warmth and affection. Do not be overly concerned if she reacts instead with indifference, resentment, or outright anger. Such reactions are common. One study of the responses of children to new siblings revealed that nearly all of them became a little naughtier, and that about half grew clingier, cried more often, or suffered toileting setbacks.

Other common negative reactions that older children may have to a new baby include demanding and difficult behavior, frequent sleep disturbances, and numerous fears. Some children become more attached to comfort objects such as pacifiers, favorite blankets, and teddy bears. Others may revert to baby talk or become more dependent on their parents in matters such as dressing and eating that once they took pride in doing entirely by themselves. Regressions of this kind are simply a child's way of reminding you that she is still little too, especially if the baby seems—in the older child's mind at least—to be guzzling all of Mommy's and Daddy's precious attention. Be understanding with her, but also be firm in insisting that the youngster resume her former behavior. Encourage her as well to express verbally any anger or resentment she might be feeling, rather than keeping it bottled up inside of her.

But negative reactions are not the invariable rule; a child's response to the baby can be positive, too. Many children respond to the new arrival by becoming more self-reliant, especially if they are recognized and praised for this kind of behavior by their parents. Others take a great interest in the newcomer, lending an eager hand with the feedings and diaperings and doing their best to keep the baby amused or comforted. Still others display increased affection for parents in the wake of the birth. But even if your child's initial reactions seem to be entirely negative, you can take comfort in knowing that they will probably be short-lived. In most cases, disruptive behavior decreases dramatically in the months following the birth as the older child gradually learns to accept her new role in the family and understands that her parents still love her every bit as much as they did before.

A toddler helping her mother with diapering feels important and grown-up. This sense of accomplishment helps keep her from engaging in the regressive behavior older children often show when an infant enters their lives.

Troubles at feeding time

Not surprisingly, older siblings are particularly likely to resent all the attention that babies get at feeding time. Your youngster may show his displeasure by misbehaving more while you are trying to breast- or bottle-feed the infant. You can eliminate some of these problems by

Mother and older child go off on an outing of their own while father and baby stay home. By finding the time to be alone with their firstborn, parents can do much to reduce feelings of jealousy toward the baby.

making the older child more a part of the routine. Lay out a snack for him, with a book or a few favorite quiet toys. Occasionally encourage him to sit next to you or to help you hold the baby's bottle. Or have him feed a doll while you feed the baby. You may also want to set up a special corner with a rocking chair for you, diapers and a change of clothing for the baby, and books, toys, puzzles, paper, and crayons for the older sibling.

The sight of his mother breast-feeding the new baby is not traumatic to the older child, as formerly believed. Your toddler may even express interest in being allowed to nurse himself. As long as you are comfortable with the notion, the best way to satisfy his curiosity is to let him try it. The chances are he will not be able to suck effectively and will not particularly like the taste even if he does manage to get some milk. Once or twice is usually enough to convince him that a sandwich and a glass of milk are a lot more satisfying and more palatable to him— and to enhance his growing pride in being a big brother. ❖

Factors Shaping Sibling Relationships

In an ideal world, the months and years following your new baby's birth would see her become—and remain—the very best of friends with her older sibling. Although many siblings do grow up together in warm and loving relationships, the world is far from perfect, and many other youngsters seem to spend much of their time together bickering and fighting. It is easy enough to understand this conflict in terms of rivalry for parental love, attention, and approval. Children do in fact jockey for position within the family hierarchy. Other causes of the conflict are less obvious, however. They are the same factors that shape a child's social development—among them the number of children in a family, their gender, their individual personalities, their birth order and age differences, the state of their health, and the sort of attachment each child has to his or her parents. These are the influences that ultimately determine the quality of relationships between siblings.

Unique personalities Even though siblings are genetically similar and grow up in the same home environment, you cannot expect them to be alike or even necessarily to like one another. The fact is, as almost any parent of two offspring will confirm, siblings may be as different in personality as unrelated children raised in different families. Interestingly, research shows that the longer siblings live together, the less alike they become. Each child is increasingly influenced by the world outside the family nest and by his desire to become an individual in his own right.

Differences in personality are perhaps the single most important variable in determining how siblings get along with each other. Most of the other variables are at least partially within your control. You can try, for instance, to determine the age gaps between your children, limit the size of your family, and with patience and understanding work to improve your relationships with your children—and theirs with each other. There is little you can do, however, to alter a child's temperament. The only option is to understand and respect each child for the unique person he is.

Birth order In one study of families with preschool-age siblings, four out of six parents described their firstborns as serious, cautious, introverted, and prone to worry or have doubts about themselves. Second children, on the other hand, were generally perceived as relatively carefree. Research that focuses on the children themselves does not bear out such generalizations. And as a result, most experts now tend to downplay the role of birth order in shaping children's personalities. It is a mistake to try to pigeonhole youngsters as more cooperative, motivated, or conformist simply because they are firstborn, or more easygoing, sociable, and freewheeling because they arrived after the first. At the same time, it does seem clear that position in the family strongly affects the way siblings relate to each other and, to some extent, to other people outside the family.

Studies show that firstborn children tend to have more ambivalent feelings about their siblings than the younger siblings have about them. The oldest children are the ones who are more likely to harbor hostility toward their rivals as they compete for parental approval and love. Underlying their resentment is the conviction that parents routinely take sides with the younger brothers or sisters. As a result, firstborns frequently prefer to play with other children rather than with their siblings. Younger children, on the other hand, generally like nothing better than playing with the oldest child.

When siblings do play together, the firstborn child tends to be controlling. To get what he wants in a dispute, he freely takes the offensive, even if it means being bossy. Although some

firstborns are physically aggressive, more often they strike out verbally with criticisms or taunts. Alternatively, a firstborn may offer bribes or use his special status as the oldest to get his way. Most younger siblings in the same situation are apt to resort to crying, pouting, pleading, or calling for help from the parents. At the same time, it is the younger siblings who are generally the most physically aggressive. They usually do not have deep-seated resentments and have not had a chance to develop hostility toward the older brother or sister. Instead of suppressing their feelings, they lash out. Most often their attacks are spur-of-the-moment, direct responses to frustration.

The impact of birth order depends to some extent on the size of the family. In a large family, the firstborn child tends to take on additional roles. Often he is protector, leader, and disciplinarian to the younger children. In a family with only two siblings, however, birth order seems to have little or no impact on relations between the children, aside from the matter of who is the boss. Feelings of love or closeness between siblings do not seem to be determined by whether a youngster is first, second, third, or thirteenth. And it is these matters—the questions of affection and support—that have the most lasting importance in shaping relationships among siblings.

The three older children in this family portrait have had to make room for a baby brother. Here the task of holding the infant has been entrusted to the only girl as a way of enhancing her new status as his big— and helpful—sister.

Gender influences   One factor that does seem to have a significant influence on personality development is the sex of your firstborn and the later siblings. Researchers have noted, for example, that many girls with older brothers are more ambitious and more aggressive than girls with older sisters. Sisters of firstborn brothers also tend to be more likely to display behavior that is tomboyish and to score higher on tests that measure intellectual ability. Boys with older brothers often tend to be more aggressive and masculine than boys with older sisters. Researchers observed that firstborn males were more susceptible to group pressure than boys with older siblings. Exactly the opposite was true of firstborn girls.

In terms of sibling relationships, gender differences have been shown to help determine how well the children will get along. In the early years, particularly, siblings of the same sex are more likely to live in harmony, while opposite-sex siblings are more prone to flare-ups and hostility. Realistically, knowing this dynamic may not help you teach your children to interact with a greater amount of love and affection, but it can help you to be more philosophical about the ongoing conflict.

The role of the parents

In addition to influencing the ways siblings interact, gender and birth order often affect the treatment that children receive from their parents. This, in turn, can have a positive or negative effect on the sibling relationship. This is particularly true when parents devote more time to one youngster.

In general, mothers and fathers are much more involved with their firstborn children than they are with the later arrivals. With no other offspring, they spend more time with the first child, talking to him more and devotedly finding ways to stimulate his development. At the same time, they lack both experience and confidence in dispatching the responsibilities of parenthood and are likely to worry more about him. They set more rules, are more rigid, and resort more often to physical punishment. Parents typically expect more from their oldest child and, frequently, more from boys than girls. Then they sometimes set unrealistically high standards for a youngster.

The arrival of the second child produces profound changes. With the increased work load of an expanding family, parents are forced to take the ups and downs of child rearing more in stride, to accept misbehavior as a passing phase and, in some instances, to bend the rules that they established for the older child. Most freely admit that they were more uptight with their first child and more relaxed with the second. They allow the later-born children more liberal bedtimes, for example, and tolerate habits such as thumb-sucking. They also approach such chores as toilet training in a far more relaxed manner.

Treating each child differently

Try as you may, it is virtually impossible to treat your children equally. It is only natural to handle them differently—to shape your parenting style to each youngster's particular needs. As one mother of six put it, "Every time I walk through the house, I have to be six different kinds of mother."

Nevertheless, in order to minimize sibling conflicts, different treatment clearly must also be fair treatment. For your oldest child this may mean a little babying now and then. It cannot hurt and may be just the thing to help him accept the pressures of being the oldest. It may also be necessary to occasionally show a little more leniency toward your firstborn and encourage him to take life less seriously. Some firstborns go overboard with the role of "good and responsible child." Likewise, it is important to devote special attention to middle children, to keep them from feeling lost in the shadow of the oldest and the light of the youngest, and to gradually dole out added responsibilities to the youngest so as not to place permanence on his privileges as "the baby in the family." Be sure that you take care, too, to discourage older siblings from teasing the youngest, yet at the same time discourage the youngest from becoming a tattletale. All the while, remember never to compare one child to another. Such commonsense measures will help ensure that all of your children receive the attention they want, the love they crave, and the approval necessary for them to thrive.

A sister lends her little brother a hand as he endeavors to fill his truck with sand. Older sisters generally prove more skillful teachers than older brothers.

Handicapped or gifted siblings

The presence of a handicapped or gifted child in the family can place extra stress on fragile sibling bonds, further complicating what is already a complex relationship. The strain can be minimized, however, by treating the special child in a natural way—without succumbing to pity for the handicapped youngster and without placing the gifted child on a pedestal. Just as with normal children, the most essential thing is to love each of your children for himself.

A child who is physically, emotionally, or intellectually handicapped will, of course, have an impact on his siblings and the relationship they share. To begin with, it is easy for parents involved with tending to the special needs of a handicapped youngster to neglect the emotional needs of the other siblings. Those children may feel left out of the family to one degree or another. It is critical, then, to make quite certain that each sibling receives a fair share of the parents' attention. Even more than in families without such complications, it may be necessary to set aside a special time for each child.

A youngster's handicap may prompt conflicting emotions on the part of the siblings. They may worry that they too might some day become handicapped or feel guilty for not sharing in the troubles of their brother or sister. As well, they may be embarrassed in

Girls with older brothers often engage in tomboyish pursuits, like this rambunctious preschooler, who gleefully shares a jungle gym with her brother.

front of their friends or resentful of the attention the handicapped child receives. In dealing with such feelings, communication is the primary requirement. You will need to be completely honest about the handicapped child's condition and encourage the siblings to air their thoughts, however negative they may be. Moreover, since your children will take most of their cues from you, make every effort to accept the handicapped child as he is and to ignore reactions of nonfamily members, even though they might be unkind.

In addition, as far as is possible, avoid putting undue pressure on siblings to care for the handicapped youngster. Instead, let each child decide for herself how involved she wants to be. You can take heart in the fact that studies have shown that siblings of handicapped children are well adjusted in most cases, and in some instances are more mature, responsible, tolerant, and altruistic than their peers.

A child with exceptional talents or intelligence can also provoke jealousies among her siblings unless parents are careful not to pay too much attention to the gifted one. As with a handicapped child, the key to preserving harmony is to enjoy the gifted one for who she is, while supporting the talents of the others. Encourage forthrightness in dealing with feelings and try to involve the siblings in the life of the exceptional child, perhaps by having them study or read together. It also helps to think of the child's giftedness as something for the entire family to enjoy and her achievements as a source of pride for all the members. Here, more than ever, avoid making comparisons between your children. And take to heart the message of the mother who once said that all of the flowers in her garden could not be roses and if they were, how monotonous that garden would be. ❖

Demonstrating a toy to his handicapped brother, this youngster displays the empathetic behavior he has learned from his parents' example. In a family with a handicapped child, the goal for all should be full acceptance of the child.

The Paradox of Rivalry and Loyalty

Siblings have been fighting with each other since time immemorial. That does not mean that nothing can be done to minimize the quarreling—in fact, a great deal can be done (*box, page 80*). First, however, it is important to realize that sibling rivalry is natural, and in most instances healthy, and second, that there is another side to the situation that too often is overlooked. This is the love and cooperativeness that also exist between most siblings, even between those who regularly fight. Researchers have been so preoccupied with the negative aspects of the relationship that they have devoted less time to studying the loyalty and solidarity that can be very much a part of a shared childhood.

A basis for friendship
For all their fighting, siblings more often than not identify with each other. As kin, they learn about the world together. And when shared experiences begin to accumulate, a sense of loyalty emerges that can deepen into a lifelong bond.

Sibling loyalty is apparent in the protective concern of brothers and sisters for one another. Many parents have seen a scolded child turn to a sibling for comfort or support—or have been surprised to find a youngster, usually critical of his rival, suddenly leap to his defense, as though some great injustice had been done. Others have seen an older sibling suddenly grab a younger brother or sister when the smaller child has gotten too close to the top of the stairs. This same protectiveness can extend beyond the home, with the older child backing up the younger one in tense or difficult play situations involving other children. Such moments of solidarity build mutual trust.

The eternal struggle
Though sibling rivalry is an inevitable feature of family life, acceptance of the fact does not mean that you will not ask yourself from time to time why your children must go on fighting. Just about every parent asks that question too. In some cases, the answer is very simple: They enjoy battling each other and see no reason to stop. In other instances, the children scrap because they may need more of your love, attention, or approval and will

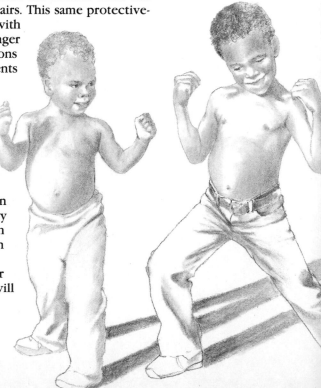

A little boy flexing his muscles shows his older brother he wants to be like him. Admiration and imitation strengthen the sibling bonds in many families.

resort to any means to get it. Jealous of one another, each wants to feel that he or she is the child you love most. Children can be very sly. Having fought his rival once in front of you and succeeded in getting your attention, a child is likely to try it again to see whether he can ensnare you a second time, especially if you can be counted on to take sides in the argument. Warring siblings like nothing better than to force you to say who you think was right and who was wrong. If you go on falling for their ploy, they will endlessly contend. Instead, accept their anger, listen to each as he expresses what he considers the reason for the conflict, and then indicate that you are confident that they will be able to work out their differences themselves.

A protective older brother escorts his sibling from a scene of rejection. Support like this helps to build strong bonds between siblings who at other times might be rivals.

Toddlers can be fast learners in the game of sibling rivalry. They may not force you to take sides, but it will not be long before they make the discovery that they can give as much as they get. One study showed that at fourteen months of age most children reacted by crying when older siblings pushed them down or took away their toys. But within four months, these same toddlers, emulating the older children's behavior, were likely to meet aggression with aggression, and were even sometimes the aggressors themselves.

While the struggle for parental attention may deeply affect the way youngsters of the same brood relate to one another, other factors can shape their behavior as well. For some children, simply living close together is enough to trigger competition for physical or emotional space in the home. The territorial imperative can make them fiercely protective of their possessions or friends. Other youngsters have a strong need to assert themselves and have their opinions heard and accepted. When that need goes unmet, they may hold their siblings to blame for getting in the way with their own views and demands. The natural tendency of some children to want to demonstrate that they are old enough to take care of themselves can put them in direct conflict with older bossy brothers and sisters.

Perils of favoritism   As might be expected, one of the greatest causes of sibling rivalry is favoritism. A survey of one group of adults revealed that of those who competed or fought with their brothers and sisters when they were children, nearly half felt that the igniting spark was their parents' apparent preference for one child over the others.

Of course, even the best of mothers and fathers will occasionally give in to the urge to compare siblings or, in a weaker moment, place one above the rest. It is not uncommon, for example, for a parent to single out a pleasant or good-looking child, or one who shares the parent's interest or talent, for special blessing. Similarly, a mother may favor her youngest child because she herself was the youngest in her family. Another may resent her oldest child because the youngster reminds her of her own shortcomings or resembles one of her siblings who antagonized her as a girl.

Whatever motivates it, favoritism only ensures resentment toward the favored youngster and toward the parent on the part of the other children in the family. An unfavored child may feel inadequate and may rebel against the very virtues that the parent so much admires in the favored child. Moreover, he may be confused by his unequal status and alienate himself further by striving doubly for the parent's love.

The favored child, too, suffers rather than benefits from his exalted position. His preferred status may prompt him to lord it over his siblings, increasing their resentment of him still more. Or, in his zeal to live up to his parents' expectations, he may become terrified of failure, fearing that he will fall from grace. It is also common for a favored child to feel guilty about monopolizing the spotlight. He might even begin purposely to curtail his accomplishments so as to shift attention away from himself. But of all the damage caused by favoritism, the worst is to have your children dislike each other, not just for now but for the rest of their lives.

Although it is quite normal to prefer one child to another, the trick is not to let your preference show. To avoid this trap, try to understand your own feelings. Why do you have a favorite? Is he more like you than his siblings? Or does he remind you of the father you loved dearly? Only by honestly answering such questions can you hope to bring the roots of your feelings to light.

For starters, learn to accept and appreciate the differences in your offspring. They are, after all, individuals in their own right and deserve to be treated as such. Take the time to get involved in the specific interests of each and involve the child in yours. At all costs, avoid making comparisons, even subtle or seemingly innocuous ones such as, "Why can't you clean up your plate like your sister?" or "You're the big brother and should know better." Children are sensitive to such remarks and resent having their siblings upheld as models for them to emulate. Besides, comparisons lead to typecasting, with perhaps one child being called responsible, the other neat, the third a clown. With such labels affixed to them, they are destined to act the part. "My parents always praised me for being the responsible one," remembers a disappointed adult, "and I lived up to their expectations. But it came at a price. To this day, my brother and sister still play helpless and I'm stuck with all the family problems."

An older child may revert to whining or clinging behavior when the demands of a baby force her to compete for parental attention. The solution: The mother will give her some time of her own later on.

"Who do you like better?" Sooner or later, one of your children is bound to ask who you love the most. The quick answer—"I love each of you the same"—is also the most fallacious. There is almost no way to love each child exactly the same. Being unique, every youngster elicits a different response from you. Likewise, absolute impartiality is impossible. It is far better to say something like, "All of you are different and I love you all differently, but I love each one of you a lot." Shared love does not mean less love.

The benefits of sibling rivalry As unpleasant as it may be at times, sibling rivalry serves a useful purpose. As Dr. Brazelton points out, it "can be a major spur in children's learning to live together, learning how to share, how to win victories and suffer defeats, how to love, and how to cope with their own unloving feelings."

While no sibling relationship should be permitted to degenerate into violence and physical or psychological abuse, it is counterproductive to deny your children the chance to work out their differences and to learn the meaning of compromise. Childhood rivalries must be resolved in childhood; otherwise, they may fester and be carried over into adulthood.

Minimizing Sibling Rivalry

Sibling rivalry may be normal, healthy, even necessary, but it is very trying for other family members, who have to share a home with the battling brothers or sisters. A certain amount of jealousy will be inevitable, especially following the arrival of a new baby. But there are many

- Teach your children to be sensitive to the needs and feelings of their siblings. When your older child makes the younger one cry, you might remind him how he felt when pushed to tears at the same age.

- Give each child at least some opportunity to feel like an only child. Set aside a special time each day for individual attention. As little as twenty minutes can have a mitigating effect on aggressive behavior. Use the time to play, read, color, or talk—any activity is fine as long as you carry it out together. If you do not have time for a special activity, simply have one child accompany you on your errands, while the other stays behind with your spouse.

- Teach your children to ask for attention in ways that you will recognize and approve of. It is far better to have your child ask you to read her a story when she needs attention than to have her make the same point by whacking the baby on the head.

- Acknowledge the accomplishments of your children and praise their cooperation. If you see your daughter share her toys with her brother, reinforce her positive act by telling her how much you appreciate it.

- Clearly lay down the law as to what you consider acceptable conduct. If there is to be no hitting, screaming, or throwing things in your home, say so—firmly—and not just once but often. And be ready to use punishment when the rules are broken. To be effective, the "no hitting" rule must apply to you as well.

- Consistently enforce your house rules. An effective punishment is "time-out." If necessary, put the battling siblings in separate locations and set a kitchen timer for two to three minutes, long enough to let them cool down. When the buzzer sounds, bring them back together to discuss the problem and consider ways to resolve it. The idea is to let the children find solutions to their own problems. Doing this will teach them to cooperate and excuses you from having to play the counterproductive role of judge and arbiter of sibling disputes.

- Make sure the older youngster has a place to retreat. A room of his own or even a corner all to himself may be just what the big brother needs when a younger sibling's pestering or toy thefts get to be too much.

- Create opportunities for constructive mutual play. Even a toddler can amuse an infant sibling by making funny faces, rolling around on the floor, or playing peek-aboo. Older children can draw or read together, play with blocks, have a tea party—the possibilities are end-

practical steps you can take to ensure that the rivalrous feelings remain within bounds. The heart of the matter in defusing conflict is to help your youngsters find positive ways of getting the attention they need. Here are a few suggestions that have been of help to other parents:

less. In the process, the younger child learns new skills by imitating her sibling, while the older child is rewarded by a growing sense of responsibility as the teacher.

- Find same-age playmates for the children. If your youngsters are fighting too much, invite over one friend for each child. Companions from outside the family will constitute a welcome and timely diversion.

- Turn a deaf ear to sibling arguments, unless they threaten to become violent. Remember, your children want your attention, and by rushing to intervene every time you hear them raise their voices, you show that you have taken their bait.

- Treat children fairly, not necessarily equally. An older child, by virtue of age, deserves privileges equal to his responsibilities. As the younger child matures, increase her responsibilites and be sure to praise the way she carries them out.

- Discourage tattling. Children assume that snitching on siblings is a good way to gain the approval of parents. It is best to ignore this ploy, unless you are being alerted to an obvious danger. When you react to tattling the first time by intervening, this almost guarantees its happening again. Let your youngster know that you do not want secondhand information about other people's behavior.

- Do not feel that you always have to get to the bottom of every dispute. Putting yourself in that position will almost inevitably leave you open to charges of favoritism. It is perfectly acceptable to simply walk away, saying: "This is your argument, and you will have to solve it yourselves."

- Do not allow children to play one parent against the other. In any given situation, one parent is likely to be more lenient than the other, and your children will quickly get to know which is which. Present a united front and do not let yourselves be manipulated.

- Encourage individuality by helping each child make the most of his particular skills and talents.

- Temporarily remove disputed toys from the scene of conflict. If your children are battling over a ball, take it away for fifteen minutes and explain to them that they can play with it later so long as they are able to share it nicely. In choosing this course of action, you are not assigning blame to either youngster, but you are still letting both know that you do not like that kind of behavior. If the fighting resumes when you give the ball back, retire it for the day.

A battle over a toy is defused when the older sister willingly relinquishes it (below). Through conflict and competition, siblings learn that they are not the center of the world, and that they must get along with others. The positive behavior of one can be an influence on the other.

When sibling rivalry gets out of hand

In some cases, however, rivalry is carried too far, reaching a point where it is destructive to the children and to the family as a whole. Left unchecked, it can destroy a youngster's self-confidence or distort his developing personality. Thus, though you will want to give your youngsters some latitude for settling problems on their own, you will also need to be alert for signs that the competition is getting out of hand. If, for example, ordinary fighting and anger turn into outright hatred and lead to physical harm, you will need to intervene.

When the struggle is consistently lopsided—with one child always the tyrant and the other the victim—or when it becomes so intense that there is no peace in the household, you may want to enlist professional help. Thankfully, such situations are relatively rare, and reason more often than not comes to prevail once the anger subsides.

What can you do to forestall rivalry?

There is, of course, no such thing as a "cure" for sibling rivalry. To deal with it, you must monitor your children's behavior and administer steady applications of love and guidance. Take comfort in the fact that the situation usually does get better as the youngsters become more mature. The chances are very good that your children will go on to build and enjoy a friendly relationship. •:•

When It's Twins

Identical twins like these generally have a close and harmonious relationship, but it is wise for parents to encourage their individual development.

Twins are on the rise. Approximately one out of every ninety births in the U.S. yields twins, and the number is increasing, largely due to the use of fertility drugs by childless couples.

For parents, twins pose enormous challenges, as well as exciting benefits. Not only is the volume of day-to-day labor formidable, but there are added complexities in fostering healthy personality development and friendly relations between the twin siblings.

It has been said that twins do not just double a mother's work, they triple or quadruple it. This certainly holds true for family relationships. Each parent must forge not one or two, but three different connections—one with each twin and another with the twins as a pair. And with other children in the family, the web of relationships expands sharply.

Parents who have raised twins successfully have many insights to share. They know how important it is to give each twin his due and spend time alone with him. In relating to their twins, they resisted the urge to think of them as a set. Instead, they made certain that each child came to appreciate his or her own uniqueness and developed the self-esteem and sense of independence needed for success in life.

On this account, giving twins rhyming names, as some people do, is not a good idea; the names may seem cute at the moment, but later in life Fay and Kay or Don and Ron may not appreciate their parents' wit. Likewise, it is not a good idea to dress twins alike, at least not all the time. Neither can they be expected to share everything as they grow older. They should be encouraged to recognize their individual likes and dislikes, to choose their own friends, and to follow their own interests. In particular, they should never be referred to as "the twins."

Special links and special problems

Not surprisingly, twins tend to have extremely close relationships. They typically spend a great deal of time together, often to the exclusion of their other siblings, and this reinforces the unique link that exists between them. While such closeness can certainly be a source of joy and security, it can also lead to a mutual dependency and may leave each of the children feeling unhappy or insecure when the two are separated. Some twins become so close that they even make up their own private language—a code of gestures, sounds, and foreign-sounding words that may seem like gibberish to others but is perfectly understandable to them. In such cases, normal language development may be delayed and a parent will have to take steps to correct the problem. The best course is to refuse to respond to the twins' requests unless they are expressed comprehensibly.

In general, identical twins like and accept each other, and—at least in the first few years—may be less prone to conflict with their nontwin siblings. They often find a natural equilibrium in their own relationship, with one twin assuming a dominant role and the other a passive one.

Fraternal twins, on the other hand, can be just as rivalrous as other siblings, sometimes even more so. This is not surprising, considering that they develop from separate ova and sperms, just like nontwin siblings. They have no more genes in common than any other brother or sister. Thus, for fraternal twins, who may find themselves widely expected to be exactly alike, there is often a strong need to assert individuality. And this is exactly the kind of pressure that children express through sibling conflict. Like identical twins, fraternal twins should be treated as separate individuals.

The needs of the others

Given the special nature of the relationship between twins, it is understandable that the other children in the family might feel they are left out. In spite of the fact that the parents are very busy after their twins are born, they should make a special effort to see that the emotional requirements of other offspring do not go ignored. And even more than in normal circumstances, parents ought to be prepared to cope with the regressions, jealousy, and anger their children may feel in response to the coming of twins into the family circle. Parents should remember that problems will arise if they talk of "the twins" and "the others." ❖

Overlooked while a neighbor admires her twin brothers, this girl withdraws. Parents can help by reminding other adults of the older child's need for attention.

Handling Stress

Life would not be life without stress, and human beings seem to have been born to cope. What family escapes the pressures of life? Were the stresses that go with being a parent not manageable, people might have given up wanting children long ago. Stress-making situations can range from the everyday demands of a toddler that leave a mother feeling stretched thin to the complications that come with having a second child, moving to a new home, or resuming a career. And then there are the crises that almost every family must face—serious illness, loss of a job, death of a loved one. All too often, stress blows worries out of proportion. Parents, in particular, tend to be hard on themselves when it comes to raising their offspring, seeking perfection in an imperfect world.

When stresses pile up, they can have a destructive effect on a family unless the members are prepared to deal with them positively. Fortunately, there is a mechanism that can keep most situations from getting out of hand or becoming desperate—love. On days when the boss has hollered at you or when just getting a casserole into the oven and onto the table can seem like a minor miracle, a consoling touch, such as the boy opposite is giving his mother, or a spouse's kiss, can work wonders. As a matter of fact, families in which members support one another emotionally find it easier to handle such common family pressures as overloaded schedules, financial problems, and arguments. This section will show you approaches you can take to relieve some of the stresses you may be experiencing in your role as a parent, including even how and when to seek professional help.

Handled constructively, the challenges posed by stress can temper family bonds. Indeed, experts have found that some families emerge from critical situations significantly stronger than they were before, better able to face the future together.

Common Family Pressures

No one is ever quite alone in her feelings. You can be certain that whatever pressure you may be feeling at the moment, someone else is also experiencing. How many parents, like the exasperated mother below, daily run up against the frustration of a child who suddenly refuses to cooperate? Such behavior can create deep tensions, especially if it goes on over an extended period of time.

There are, to be sure, innumerable stress-making situations in family life. In one study, two-parent families and single mothers both name anxiety over money as the number one source of their day-to-day stress. Conflicts related to child rearing and sharing household responsibilities also rank high on any list of common family stresses. In addition, couples frequently mention concerns about sexual relations as yet another pressure in their lives. And nearly everyone, it seems, feels the need for more privacy, more time to spend relaxing.

As families develop and change, they tend to work out systems of their own for dealing with their everyday problems. There is perhaps no one right way to handle any of the common pressures, and each family's solution is bound to be slightly different, some more effective than others. Nonetheless, there are a few basic attitudes and approaches that can help family members pull together as they cope with the wear and tear of life. Developing these is usually a matter of finding the family's strengths, then building upon them.

The myth of the perfect family Who has not imagined the perfect family? Mother, father, and children all take one another's needs into account and have loving relationships that forestall arguments and keep the world at bay. Mom holds down a high-level job, yet still has energy left over to cook a good meal, nurture her youngsters, and relate to her husband. Dad, too, manages to be a go-getter

in his profession, an enthusiastic parent, and an all-round good sport. In this mythical family, the children are always achievers—and, of course, when they grow up they become immensely successful.

Tested against reality, this image of the perfect family proves fantasy. However unrealistic the notion may be, the pursuit of perfection causes much of the stress felt by many of today's families as they strive to achieve the dream that must forever be beyond them.

You yourself may have several unrealistic expectations for your own family. If you do, you may want to sit down and do some hard thinking about what is truly important to you and what is not, and let your other aspirations go, at least for the time being. These measures will not magically wipe away all the problems of being a parent. Stresses and conflicts will be many and varied: Toddlers and preschoolers are bound to be rebellious on occasion, a spouse may be distracted by pressure at work, and the roof may have sprung a leak in the last rainstorm. But if you are prepared for such eventualities, they will be far easier to bear when they arise.

Respecting her mother's desire for privacy, this girl has been taught to knock on a door before entering. A chance to be alone, even briefly, can serve as a restorative for a frazzled parent's nerves.

Family communication The strength to cope springs from many sources. Not least of these is being honest with yourself and being able to bring up and discuss feelings—both positive and negative—with the family. Members who trust one another and who are able to speak their minds freely are more resilient when facing stress than those who avoid talking about difficulties. If possible, build this kind of open exchange not only with your mate and offspring, but also with your extended family. And never forget that communication need not be verbal in order for you to get the right message across—a hug can be a statement too.

When it comes to airing a grievance, try to state your feelings clearly and reasonably. Avoid blaming your child or spouse and resist turning a disagreement into a power struggle. Instead, approach the situation with the aim of finding a solution that will be satisfactory not only to you but

Her patience stretched, a busy mother tries to get her uncooperative child to go with her on a shopping expedition. Children's difficult behavior is a major stress-maker for parents.

also to the others concerned. Naturally, there will be times when you and your mate must agree to disagree, or when you tell your child he must obey you despite his preferences, but try to be open-minded and flexible. It helps reduce tensions in a family dispute, for example, to offer an occasional supportive, nonjudgmental response, such as "I see what you mean" or "That sounds very important to you"—and mean it.

How parental disputes affect a child

Many parents feel uneasy about disagreeing or arguing in front of a child. Certainly, if the fight is vituperative, the youngster is not going to benefit from being present—indeed, it is likely to frighten him. But in a loving family, arguments generally do not turn nasty. It is better to let your child see you fighting, even if it upsets him, than to have him experience the unspoken hostility that can linger after an argument. When you and your spouse go about the house tight-lipped or with false smiles, your child will pick up on the negative emotions that lie hidden just beneath the surface. And when such contrived good will is prolonged, the child will begin to mistrust his own perceptions; this can be damaging to his growing sense of reality.

In most cases, therefore, it is wiser for you and your partner to allow the youngster to witness the quarrel than to end it abruptly and unnaturally. As a matter of fact, seeing parents argue constructively can help a child understand that her own feelings of anger are normal and that it is safe for her to express them.

In the heat of an argument, it may be hard for you to take your listening child into account, but if you can let her know why Mommy and Daddy are fighting, you all will be the better off for it. While arguing, you might interject something like "We're having an argument, but we'll figure it out," or "Just because we're angry doesn't mean we don't love each other." And when it is over, reassure your child that she was in no way the cause of the disagreement, since children often make the assumption assume that somehow

Bending to listen, a mother takes into account her son's protest over having to go out with her rather than play with his fort. Good family communication involves accepting negative as well as positive behavior.

they are to blame. Let her know that all is well again—you might suggest a family activity to show her that family ties are strong enough to withstand altercations. But nothing can offer better proof of this than a make-up kiss between the parents—with a kiss for the child too.

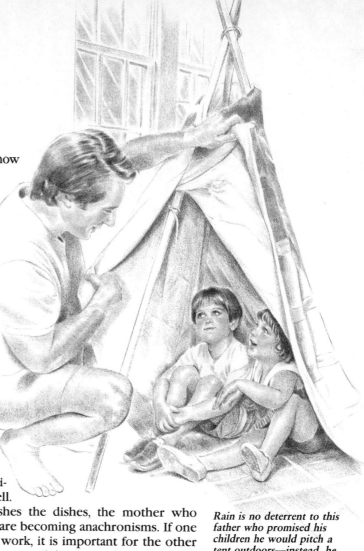

Flexibility and individuality

Essential to handling pressure in a family is flexibility. The members need to be able to adapt to change and to accommodate the needs of all; they also should be willing to experiment with different approaches to problems. Flexibility extends to roles as well. The father who never washes the dishes, the mother who refuses to fix a leaky faucet are becoming anachronisms. If one spouse is unusually busy at work, it is important for the other to assume some additional responsibilities. So too a youngster can be of help; the one who learns to take care of his own playthings and to perform simple mealtime chores is a valuable family member.

New responsibilities increase each family member's sense of independence and self-esteem, especially when contributions are recognized and appreciated by all. But they should not be developed at the expense of any one person's individuality. Families that deal well with stress, experts have found, are close but allow each member to be a distinct personality.

Rain is no deterrent to this father who promised his children he would pitch a tent outdoors—instead, he has set it up in the living room. Being flexible, he has prevented their disappointment and won some peace for himself.

Enjoying family life

Such families have no inhibitions about showing happiness and joy. Having a good time together can go a long way toward reducing stress; sharing pleasurable experiences leaves everyone feeling good. A bit of humor now and then pays handsome rewards: As all but the humorless know, laughter has a way of reducing problems to manageable proportions. ⁘

When You Get Angry at Your Child

All parents at one time or another become furious with their children. But some know how to handle their anger and others are afraid of the damage they might do releasing it. Far from being a sign that you do not love your child, expressing anger toward him can be a measure of just how much you really care for him. But because the balance of power is so heavily weighted in the adult's favor, it is important to retain some self-control when giving vent to your irritations. Following are tips to help you deal with your anger constructively.

● Do not do a slow boil. Admit to yourself that you are angry and then pause for a long moment to pinpoint the cause. Ask yourself, "What do I see or hear that is making me so angry?"

And then, "What can I do about it?"

● Think in terms of finding a solution to the specific situation that has aroused your ire. Instead of dwelling on your child's shortcomings, ask yourself what kind of behavior you would prefer.

● Now tell your child exactly what has displeased you. Address the immediate occasion for your anger; do not criticize your child's personality or review her past behavior. And by no means compare her to other children.

● Allow the child to express her feelings too, and acknowledge them.

● Describe the behavior you would like to see—"You may cross this street only with an adult holding your hand."

And then when the child conforms, praise her for it.

● Keep confrontations brief. Return to pleasant interactions with your youngster as soon as they seem natural. Do not bear grudges. Chances are your child will forget the incident a lot sooner than you will.

● After you have been firm on an issue, do not give in to guilty feelings and contradict your own discipline by backing off. Children quickly learn to take advantage of a guilty and vacillating parent.

● If you find it all but impossible to express your anger overtly and instead feel continually hostile toward your child, seek help to find out why.

When Your Child Gets Angry at You

A young child's anger at a parent can be intense, for there are many frustrations in being small and dependent. Indeed, it can be so strong that the child may find the emotion frightening; after all, he is directing it at the people he loves and needs most. It is important, however, that he be able to express his anger constructively and to learn that the parent-child bond can weather his fury. Here are ways to help him:

● Make every effort to remain calm.

● Look for the cause of your child's anger. In finding it, you may be able to do something about it. Remember that his irritability may have more to do with his being tired or hungry, or with his coming down with an illness, than with any deep-seated cause.

● Help the child communicate anger verbally, by suggesting words and phrases for feelings.

● Be forbearing when your child's words hurt your feelings. Many angry children tell their parents "I hate you" or "I want to kill you." Remember that your child is venting rage; his words do not mean he does not love you. Nevertheless, he should not be allowed to think that he can insult or hurt you any time he pleases.

● Teach your child to tell you why he is furious at you. A child who says that he is going to run away, for example, can be told, "I see that you are very angry with me. I can listen to whatever is making you angry—you don't have to run away."

● If the youngster is old enough to understand, help him distinguish between emotions and deeds. Explain that the feeling of wanting to kill someone is quite different from actually doing it.

● Draw some limits on the child's anger. If your preschooler's rage gets out of hand, put him in a time-out, a brief but effective period by himself spent in some neutral place where you can watch him. Here he can recover his composure.

● When he is calm, show your child that he can resume his regular behavior without losing face. When he reappears after a tantrum, you might suggest a pleasurable activity to do together.

Preventing Parental Burnout

Parental burnout is aptly named, for it occurs primarily when parents run out of emotional fuel, especially when they have difficulty fulfilling their many roles. Studies show that women are more prone to burnout than men, largely because they continue to shoulder more of the responsibilities of home and family. It is they who suffer more of burnout's common symptoms—fatigue, depression, and frequent minor physical complaints, such as colds and backaches; loss of sexual desire is another. Before you begin to feel this way, consider some preventive measures.

There is, of course, nothing more immediately effective than the occasional good break. But plan for it; otherwise you are not likely to find time to take it when you need it.

To give yourself time, see whether you can get some help for yourself, either by asking friends or relatives to lend you a hand or by hiring a cleaning person, a baby-sitter, a teenager to cut the grass. (But when you have someone else do a chore for you, resist applying your standards to the other's performance.)

If you have a full-time job, end the afternoon with ten minutes of reflection about the day's events, so that you can get up and leave the office behind you. To reduce the stress of a too-busy life, look into the possibility of flextime or job-sharing. Flextime allows an employee to set her own hours as long as she meets a weekly requirement; job-sharing permits two people to hold one job, each working part-time.

Prevent pressures from building up. Temporarily put aside some of your aspirations and resist becoming overcommitted to community or office. Indulge yourself occasionally: Go to bed right after dinner, relax with a good book, take a leisurely walk. Or from time to time vary the patterns of family life: Have a picnic on a blanket in the living room in the dead of winter, take the family one night to a formal restaurant instead of the usual fast-food restaurant.

Adopt a long-range view. Look ahead, not just a week or a month at a time, but well into the future. In a quiet moment sit down with your spouse and together make some major life decisions, such as when to have another child, shift jobs, or move to a bigger house. But be sure to stagger these to avoid magnifying the stress that goes with change.

Of all the things you can do, perhaps there is none more important than taking good care of yourself. Eating properly, exercising regularly, and getting sufficient sleep may not reduce stress, but they do provide the energy and resilience you must have in order to cope effectively. ❖

Weathering a Crisis

The test of a family's resiliency is the way it responds to and handles a crisis. During a difficult period, routines go by the board, roles are changed or reversed, and the members must carry on under trying or unusual circumstances for days or even months. The causes vary widely—running the gamut from death to other calamities such as hurricanes and floods. Positive events can put families under pressure too. The birth of a child causes disruptions and realignments; a promotion can provoke anxiety as well as joy.

Whatever precipitates a turning point in family life, however, the result is usually dynamic. The challenged family learns to cope, if it does not already know how. The family that can pull together during turbulent times is likely to emerge with its members committed anew to each other—and more deeply appreciative of themselves as a dynamic unit.

How families react to crisis

Often, the first reaction to a crisis is numbness and denial—refusal to believe that a loved one has died, for example, or that a spouse has a serious mental problem or an incurable illness. This is only natural: People need to readjust, and it is hard to deal with excessive pain and worry all at once. But after the shield has fallen away, a period of emotional intensity may follow—sadness, anger, resentment, and loneliness can all well up. For a while, it may seem as though life will never return to normal. But then, as is so often the case, a family discovers resources it did not know it had.

Tackling the unexpected

Many of the attitudes and habits that help families accept common, daily pressures are key to their handling more traumatic events as well. If the members already communicate honestly, directly, and openly, they will be better able to discuss the emotions and practical concerns that come with crisis. Being adaptable, too, enables them to swap roles as necessary and to adjust to new schedules. And finally, those who are accustomed to making decisions together and sharing responsiblities will be better able to do so during extraordinary times, when mutual support is needed as never before.

Such a family is also able to reach out to friends, relatives, and the community for support when the necessity arises. Since asking for help could be seen as a sign of weakness, some families refuse to even ask. But it is the strong family that can ask for—and accept—help. Relatives, friends, and neighbors are usually more than willing to provide meals for a family in distress. They are also likely to provide a sympathetic ear. Many have gone through similar experiences and are happy to offer help by sharing their insights.

Finally, attitude plays a major role in the way a family handles a crisis. You do not have to be a Pollyanna—or deny negative feelings—to believe that a family can be renewed by struggle.

Helping your child cope
When events put the family on temporarily shaky ground, a small child is bound to feel insecure and confused. Children depend on routine, and crisis usually means that it is interrupted. Thus a parent should try to restore the child's own schedule as soon as possible. And if life is going to be confusing for several weeks, the mother or father should establish a few anchors—a quiet conversation over cereal in the morning, a happy story before lights-out.

It also is important to assure a toddler or preschooler—verbally and with hugs and kisses—that she will be cared for as before; when disorder reigns, a child will naturally fear for her own well-being and perhaps even fantasize that she will be abandoned. She should be told that although life is chaotic right now, she is as much loved as ever. She should also be told why things have changed, and then, when the information has sunk in, she should gently be invited to talk about her reactions.

When illness strikes
The serious illness of a parent or child inevitably disrupts family routine, often for weeks or even months. Visits to the doctor, hospital stays, and in-home care must somehow be woven into the fabric of daily life. Uncertainty about the outcome of the illness adds a large measure of anxiety to a household, especially when a member of the parenting team is the patient involved.

If your spouse falls seriously ill, you may well have some reactions that are not strictly sympathetic. It is natural to feel some resentment toward the person who has left you to cope on your own, and, at the same time, it is usual to feel both guilty and relieved that you were not stricken. In addition, when the illness is truly severe, you may have private thoughts about your spouse's death, trying to imagine what life would be like without him. Denying such thoughts does no good; a feeling of guilt often arises when they are not squarely faced. This does not mean, of course, that you need express them aloud; accepting them as natural should help you get a grip on them.

Your child will have distinct reactions to the illness, too. Along with worrying that her own misbehavior or aggressive thoughts may have caused the parent to fall ill, she almost

certainly will feel vulnerable. As she senses your distraction, she may become more demanding than usual, or she may try to be on her best behavior at all times, hoping by this to work some magic cure on the patient. Since her imagination can run in strange directions at such times, it is up to you to put her at ease about her troubling thoughts and to point out reality.

A younger sister's illness produces a sympathetic response from an older brother, who entertains her with finger puppets. Children can play helpful roles when siblings become sick.

Aiding a child's adjustment

First and foremost, reassure your child that you, her healthy parent, are strong and well and will continue to care for her. Tell her that her life will go on as before, despite your spouse's illness. Next, explain what the illness is, naming the condition or disease and outlining its effects simply and clearly. Be sure to let the youngster know what its course is likely to be.

As part of her adjustment, provide opportunities for your youngster to play with others of her age. Children who must live with a sick parent can miss out on many childhood pleasures. They become overly serious and sometimes refuse to leave the house, for fear of abandoning the needy parent. Reassure your child that it is not her responsibility to take care of the patient. If your spouse's illness permits, allow your child to have friends come play with her at home; if not, arrange for her to visit them frequently. And, unless you have good reasons not to want her to say anything, encourage the child to talk about the illness with them.

The threat of divorce

While a parent's illness may be threatening to a youngster, it does not destroy the bonds between parent and child. Divorce, on the other hand, can appear to some children to sever these important links. Certainly a youngster will not be happy to hear that the two people she loves and needs most are splitting up— but she can emerge from the experience with her sense of self intact and her love for her parents as great as ever, if both spouses keep her needs and concerns in mind.

Explaining the reasons for the breakup

Divorcing parents should sit down with their youngster to inform her of their decision; this allows her to see that the choice is a mutual one. They should explain clearly and simply what is going to happen and why, stating the reasons for the breakup. They should also tell her where the parent who is moving out will live. Most of all, they should do everything possible to reassure her that she has done nothing to contribute to the breakup. As with the youngster who lives with a seriously ill family member, a child of divorcing parents will often blame herself. In any case, her reaction is likely to be one of sadness and of anger, and here again she will need the understanding and love of mother and father. Preschoolers are especially vulnerable and may resort to infantile behavior, become unusually fearful, or act the bully with friends.

Alone at the door, the son of divorced parents waits for his father to pick him up for a weekend outing. The noncustodial parent's involvement with the child is crucial to the youngster's development.

Adjusting to divorce

After a divorce, both parents and child must assume new roles and new routines. A mother may have to return to work to supplement family income; a father may have to learn a wide range of household tasks. Probably a youngster will have some new responsibilities, too, and will have to adjust to the fact that his parents now live in separate places and that he must spend time in each.

To prevent unnecessary upset, the custodial parent will want to keep home life calm and consistent, so that the youngster will have a secure base. This means avoiding arguing with the other parent in front of the child or over the telephone when the child is nearby. It also means not using her as a go-between or asking her to take sides. And neither spouse should use the divorce as an excuse for lack of firm, fair discipline. If possible, the parents should use the same discipline approach so as not to confuse the youngster.

When death comes

The divorce of parents, however upsetting it may be to the youngster, does not have the finality about it that death does. Death shuts a door completely; those who survive must adjust to the fact that their hopes for a fulfilling life with the departed one have vanished forever. Sudden loss must be coped with, but when a family member has a terminal illness, a child can be prepared for the inevitable. He should be told soon enough to allow him to come to grips with his feelings and let him spend time with the loved one as much as is possiblc.

Painful though death is, it frequently has the effect of drawing the bereaved closer together. When made aware of the fragility of human ties, a stricken family may find itself striving all the harder to keep them strong.

A dead bug fascinates two boys. One way children learn about death firsthand is through nature. A parent should take pains to describe death as a natural part of life.

A child's view of death

When a close family member dies, a child should not be protected from knowledge of what is going on or left out of rituals that others may think are too grown-up for her. Even a toddler can understand that death is the opposite of being alive. A child deserves a simple, straightforward explanation of the loss of a loved one. In telling her about the death, the parent should hold her close and look her in the eyes. If you find yourself in such a situation, explain that, for whatever reason—illness, an accident, old age—the loved one is no longer able to think, breathe, or move. Tell her what will happen to the body now—that it will be buried or cremated—and assure her that the deceased cannot feel any pain or sadness.

Be sure to keep your language literal and your description brief and straightforward—comparing death to sleep or a long journey will conjure up all kinds of false images in the child's mind. If you have religious beliefs concerning death and an afterlife, include these in your explanation, but do not tell your child anything you yourself do not believe.

Should a child attend the funeral?

A youngster old enough to understand a simple description of a funeral should be present at this farewell ritual, unless of course he does not want to attend. His attendance will help him to understand that the person is truly gone and will make him feel important enough to have been included. Explain beforehand what to expect and that the rite is a way of saying good-bye. If for some reason your child cannot be present, make certain to leave him behind in the care of someone whom he likes and trusts.

Offering reassurances

Naturally, the youngster who has lost a parent will need to be reassured that he will continue to be cared for and loved. The surviving parent should remind him that he or she is healthy and does not expect to die for many years to come—not until the child himself is an adult, perhaps with a family of his own. At the same time, the parent should not attempt to conceal his or her own grief in front of the child—tears are essential to true mourning. In turn, the child should be allowed to demonstrate his own sorrow; it does no good to tell him that he must be a big boy now and be brave. Since he may have his own way of grieving, it is essential to let him express his feelings as he sees fit. With the love and reassurance of the surviving parent, as well as the support of other members of the family, he can adjust to the loss without trauma.

Death of a sibling

Because children identify so strongly with each other, a youngster may find the death of a sibling alarming, sometimes viewing it as a threat to her own life. Additionally, she may feel left out as her parents deal with their pain. However grieved they may be, they should make every effort to help the child cope with the situation. She has as much adjusting to do as they. By no means should they idealize the dead sibling—or become overly protective of the living child. Instead, the departed child should be talked of in a natural way, and the one who survived told that, like her parents, she will live for many years—the family will go on. ❖

As her mother gently pats her on the shoulder, a girl puts flowers on a grandmother's grave. Visiting a grave can help a child accept death's finality.

How Others Can Lend Support

In a close-knit family there is always someone to fall back on, someone to listen to a vexing problem and give advice. But there may be times when it is better to go outside for help. Experts also say that those families that accept this reality generally come through the wear and tear of life more gracefully than those whose members see asking for any kind of help beyond the immediate family as a sign of weakness. Some families may even fly in the face of reality and steadfastly deny to themselves that anything is wrong.

An evening of hashing over a problem with a friend or a series of meetings with a peer group can provide an excellent outlet for tensions and offer an objective view of your dilemma. And, in listening to others describe their problems, you may gain new insight into yours. Furthermore, in talking with others who share similar pressures, you will find that you are neither alone nor unique. The act of reaching out for support can do much to restore and enhance self-esteem.

Help can come in many forms—from loose-knit, spontaneously formed neighborhood support groups to more structured family therapy sessions. Churches, schools, hospitals, and community agencies all are involved in the effort to assist families when they need it.

Peer groups

Peer groups generally are formed to address particular concerns—those of new parents, for instance, or families dealing with an elderly parent. Sometimes new mothers and fathers in a neighborhood will get together to form their own support group. More commonly, groups are founded and sponsored by community agencies, which put an educator, a mental health professional, or a specially trained volunteer in charge.

As their name suggests, peer groups are made up of equals who talk and listen to one another in an effort to find solutions to common problems. Within the comforting security of a group, the members can say what they like, and this alone can do much to reduce stress.

Family therapy

For specific family problems that are harder to solve, it is sometimes wise to turn to one-on-one therapy or to family therapy, a counseling process that generally focuses on the family as a unit. The therapist may be a social worker, psychologist, or psychiatrist. He or she may be in private practice or work with a community agency or institution and, as a professional, must be licensed by the state to practice.

During family therapy, the therapist and family members

work together to uncover the events in the family's history and examine the day-to-day occurrences and feelings that exacerbate the particular problem. It can take courage for people to face their problems squarely. Discussions can become heated as truths and emotions are laid bare, but the net results are bound to be positive, with family ties strengthened rather than strained by mutual understanding and growth. ❖

An Expert's View

When—and Where—to Go for Professional Help

Stress comes to everyone, sometimes producing symptoms that may need attention if they are not to become worse. Symptoms can range from the obvious to the subtly complex. Knowing when to seek the kind of professional help that will provide relief depends to a large extent upon what the symptoms are and how long they have been going on. In an overstressed adult, for example, sudden difficulties in falling and staying asleep often rise out of suppressed conflicts. Hostility, mood swings, depression, apathy, suspiciousness, extreme anxiety, nervousness are all signs of disturbance that need to be be taken into account. Less obvious symptoms of mental upset, such as frequent minor illnesses like flu and colds, should be noted as well.

Children can manifest many of these same symptoms. However, they are more likely to show the effect of stress in the sudden onset and persistence of regressive behavior — bedwetting, thumb-sucking, regular tantrums, clinginess. Recurring nightmares may mirror inner strife. Similarly, excessive, fearful questioning may be motivated by pervasive anxiety. For example, after a conflict-laden divorce, a youngster might become obsessed, say, with the notion that storms bring disaster and ask multiple questions relating to them. "Will lightning strike us?" "What happens if the house floods?" "When is

it going to stop snowing?" Such questioning is a disguise for the anxiety he is experiencing about himself and his fears of abandonment.

Since a healthy person may temporarily display one or several of these symptoms, especially during times of stress, it is important to observe their intensity and to determine whether they continue over an extended period of time. Children will often regress in response to a stress, for example, but then return to more mature behavior when the provoking circumstances change or the parents are able to offer reassurance and love; only when the regressions persist should there be cause for concern.

Generally speaking, if the symptoms of disturbance in child or adult have not gone away after four or five weeks, competent intervention is called for. If nothing else, a professional will determine whether the symptoms are transitory, and so reassure you. In any case, by addressing the problems early enough, you are taking preventive measures that can pay off in relief — and in years of good mental health.

When it comes to finding help, most people do not know where to turn and often try to muddle through on their own instead. Some may be so frightened of admitting vulnerability that they begin to deny that they have a problem. Actually, finding help is not difficult. You can start by asking your physician for

referrals. You can even turn to the professional section of the telephone book and look under such categories as "Counseling," "Psychotherapy," "Child," "Family," and "Parents." You may prefer to get in touch with your church or synagogue to see whether it can help. The YWCA, YMCA, Red Cross, local hospitals, and other organizations, including colleges and universities, often have programs of their own. Alternatively, consult your county or city social service agency to see whether it offers counseling.

For marital or family problems, you may wish to write to the American Association for Marriage and Family Therapy, 1717 K St. N.W., Washington, D.C. 20006. Ask for a list of qualified counselors in your own area.

Whatever you do, review the sources you accumulate and pick a couple whose focus and qualifications seem appropriate to you. Then seek out the organizations or professionals; an initial interview will tell you what form the treatment will take—and whether the people involved are ones you can like and trust. By taking the major first step of directing someone to a professional or going yourself, you will prevent far greater problems from developing down the line.

Charles R. Figley, Ph.D.
Professor of Family Therapy
Purdue University

5 The Family Redefined

Ask a child to describe a family, and he will tell you that it consists of a mother, a father, and their children. Ask a child to describe his own family, and the answer may be quite different. Perhaps he will tell you that he lives with his mother and sees his father on weekends, or that he has a stepfather and a stepmother as well as a father and a mother. He may even tell you that he was adopted by his parents or that he is a foster child.

While the traditional nuclear family is perceived to be strong and prevalent, in reality patterns of family structure in America are far more diverse. Increasing numbers of children are spending their early years in single-parent families or with parents who have remarried. The cultural makeup of the nuclear family itself is also changing with the growing rate of interethnic, interfaith, and interracial marriages.

Children can thrive in all kinds of families, as long as there is trust, acceptance, and love. Yet single parents, along with stepparents, adoptive and interracial mothers and fathers, know that they face special challenges in raising their children.

This chapter examines the special child-rearing issues that confront nontraditional families. Happily, some of these families—like the one pictured at right —find ways to transform the source of their problems into their biggest asset. From their differences they derive their vibrancy and strength.

Single-Parent Families

One of every five preschoolers in the U.S. lives in a household in which only one parent is present. In previous generations, such single-parent families were usually brought about by the death or desertion of a parent. Today the single-parent family is more often created through separation and divorce. In many cases, the parent not living with the children is still very much a part of the picture. Even with the support of a former spouse, however, living alone with children is invariably a strenuous existence, and it can be a source of emotional problems for parents and children alike. On the positive side, many single parents find that they come to enjoy particularly close and rewarding relationships with their offspring.

Unique characteristics of the single-parent family

While the goals of single parents are the same as those of married couples raising children—to nurture, educate, and protect their offspring—their relationships with the children tend to take on distinctive qualities. In a two-parent family, the mother and father run the household jointly, backing each other up, establishing mealtimes, bedtimes, and family rules. Often, they do not even consult the children in planning day-to-day matters. The single parent—a mother here, for the sake of example—does not have the luxury of sharing decisions with another adult. No matter how energetic she may be, she faces the burden of responsibility alone. She is a loving mother

Who's Raising the Children?

The chart at right shows the living arrangements of the 21.5 million children in the U.S. under the age of six. The most significant trend reflected in these percentages is the growth in the number of single-parent families, which have doubled since 1970, due primarily to the increased rate of divorce. More men today are gaining custody of their children, but the proportion of fathers raising children alone has remained fairly constant.

Of the children living with two parents, one of every eight lives with a natural parent and a stepparent, according to Census Bureau estimates. Adopted children living in two-parent homes are included in this same category, while children living with other relatives or foster parents make up the category called "foster care."

Two parents 76.1%

Mother only: 20%

Father only: 2.1%

Foster care: 1.8%

first, but she also has bills to pay, doctors to visit, play dates to arrange, schedules to keep and, often, a full-time job outside the home.

Frequently, her response is to turn to the children for help. She tries to instill the sense that the family is "in this together." She expects the children to help around the house and to accept extra responsibility. She also lets them become her main source of support and love, her companions, and her buffer against loneliness. In return, she gives them unusual rights, such as a larger voice in family decisions.

None of this is necessarily bad—the family may develop a sense of common cause that is unusual in two-parent households. But it is clearly different from the accepted two-parent definition of family roles, and it has to be approached with a clear understanding of the potential problems.

A single mother, departing for work, plants a kiss on her toddler's cheek. Most single parents depend on a network of outside support—play group, day-care center, helpful relatives, even obliging neighbors.

A balancing act   Raising a child in a single-parent family is a delicate balancing act. It is quite easy, for example, to let anxiety about the child's welfare turn into overprotectiveness. At the playground, you may find yourself fighting the urge to restrain your toddler when he wants to strike out on his own. It is also easy to want more of the youngster's time than he may be prepared to give. If you are a working parent, you may jealously guard the time you set aside to play with your child. But in your desire to keep the youngster close to you, you run the risk of stiffling his essential instincts for independence. Moreover, no matter how intimate a relationship you may share with your child, you should be wary of relying on the youngster for emotional support. Children simply are unable to be replacements for the spouse who is missing.

Disciplining a child is always difficult. It is easier to give in to demands than to weather a youngster's tantrums. And you will be much more apt to be overly compliant if you are habitually tired or have pangs of guilt about the limited number of hours you can share with your child. The dynamics of the single-parent family, with its emphasis on pulling together, makes exercising parental authority even harder. Punishing your child fragments, however briefly, the sense of partnership that you may come to rely upon; it may even leave you feeling isolated. But a healthy, well-functioning family, whether it includes one parent or two, has to have clear-cut boundaries between the generations. You need to give your child the security of knowing that you are the one who is in charge.

Soccer coach, tutor, cook, chauffeur, disciplinarian, comforter, and much more—the single parent plays many roles in the complicated drama of parenthood. The problem is that she rarely escapes center stage.

The child's other parent

Children of divorce will generally profit from regular contact with the parent not living at home. Even if your relationship with your ex-spouse is cool or hostile, it is vital to encourage your former partner to play an active role with the children. Try to think of your mate not as an ex-spouse but as a coparent.

Right after a divorce, your child will need help not only in getting used to the idea of the family's living apart, but also in accepting the fact of having two places to stay. When a toddler first goes to spend time with her other parent, she may be fearful because she does not really understand that she will be returning to your care. She may have trouble sleeping at one or both homes and may cry when she is separated from you. Sometimes it is helpful to have your ex-spouse pick the youngster up at a neutral place, such as her day-care center. And it's always wise to encourage the child to take along any particularly favored toy, blanket, or some other special security object.

Whatever your child's age, you will want to avoid criticizing your former partner in the youngster's presence or trying to impose your feelings on her. Let her talk about her visits with the other parent, but be careful not to pry. And be prepared for critiques and comparisons by the child if her two households differ markedly from each other, particularly as far as discipline and rules are concerned. Address these differences in a straightforward manner: "That is how Daddy does things in his home, but here your bed-time is at eight o'clock." Try to reach some understanding with your former spouse in order to minimize the differences in rules or styles of discipline.

If you do not have employment outside the home, you face nearly structureless days and may quickly feel hemmed in by the endless rounds of chores and the persistent demands of your children. If you work, running a home alone while holding down a job can leave you feeling burned out. While your child is an infant or toddler, life may be especially hard because small children are in constant need of so much attention. The challenge is to find ways to meet both your child's needs for you and your own need for rest, privacy, and peace of mind.

Tending to your own needs

The place to start is in developing a support system outside the home. Where do you turn when you feel that you are at your wit's end or cannot take another minute of your child's whining over your inability to take him to the park? At such times family, friends, and even neighbors can provide relief, giving you the chance to unburden yourself; they may be able to provide some spur-of-the-moment baby-sitting as well. Knowing other parents in similar predicaments can also be a big help. You can try making an arrangement with each other, so that you both wind up having some free time of your own, away from your children. Sometimes single parents move in together in order to lighten their loads and share the responsibilities of household chores.

No matter how tight your budget, it helps to splurge occasionally. Going out for a meal or a movie, or spending money to get your hair cut or your nails done, can make you feel special and relieve some of the emotional overload. Take a few minutes every day—even if it is only ten—to read the newspaper or catch up on the mail while your child is still awake. Tell her that this is your special time and that you appreciate her for keeping busy while you have it.

Resuming your social life

A worrisome issue for many recently divorced parents is how to spare the child's feeling when you begin dating again. In part, this may be a problem of overcoming guilt about leaving the child behind, even if it is only for an evening. A practical solution is to see to it that your child has something to look forward to—a favorite baby-sitter, for example.

If you decide to entertain in your home, your child may show off or look for ways to disrupt your evening. Such behavior is understandable since, in the child's eyes, your date is a threat to her relationship with you. But, obviously, it cannot be tolerated. The best approach is to carefully prepare your child for the guest's visit, telling her exactly what the three of you will be doing together and what is expected of her. And be sure to praise her good behavior afterward.

Having a lover spend the night presents a unique set of problems. When your child confronts your friend across the breakfast table, you have brought the youngster into your new relationship. Keep in mind that the child is bound to have some sort of fantasy about your friend as the relationship develops. If you break off the relationship, your child will be affected too; he may like the individual, see him as a substitute parent, and feel something bordering on personal rejection as that person goes out of his life.

Managing the single-parent home

In the long run, the biggest hurdles that you will have to clear will be the simple realities of daily life. The crucial thing is to carefully establish your priorities. If you want to spend more time with your children and less time cleaning house, then you may need to settle for a slightly less orderly home. Keep track of the chores that really have to get done and try to follow a schedule. If you can afford it, hire someone to help you with the housework.

Whether you head off each morning to the office or stay home with your children, you have to face up to one reality of single parenthood: No matter how hard you try, you cannot completely replace a two-parent team. Your attempts at being a supermom or superdad are bound to fall short of complete success. Managing well as a single parent is more than anything a matter of practical arrangements and keeping a positive attitude. Ultimately, all that is required is your loving best. ⋰

Divorce and Remarriage

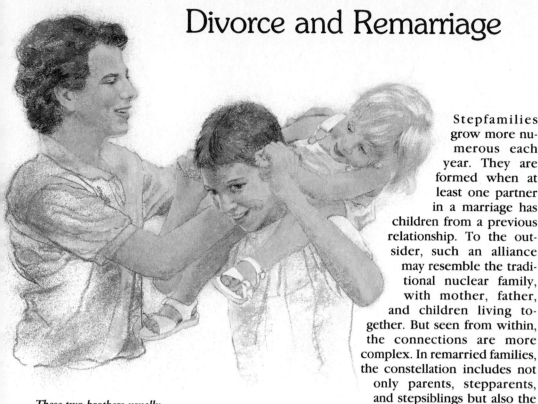

These two brothers usually prefer tennis to toddlers— their half-sister is the exception. A baby born to remarried parents often works wonders in bringing unity to the stepfamily.

Stepfamilies grow more numerous each year. They are formed when at least one partner in a marriage has children from a previous relationship. To the outsider, such an alliance may resemble the traditional nuclear family, with mother, father, and children living together. But seen from within, the connections are more complex. In remarried families, the constellation includes not only parents, stepparents, and stepsiblings but also the children's other biological parent and perhaps even stepgrandparents, grandparents, and an assortment of aunts, uncles, and cousins, related by marriage if not by blood. The picture is further complicated when the children live part-time in the new household and part-time with their other parent.

This remarried family is apprehensive about the present and the future. The children may still have a sense of unhappiness over the breakup of the previous family. As they are adjusting to their new situation, they have to resolve conflicting loyalties to their mother, their father, and the new stepparent. Because so many feelings and sensitivities are involved, it will take time for them and everyone else in the newly constituted family to sort out roles and to grow used to one another.

Becoming a stepfamily

Since the implications of bringing two families together under one roof are many, anyone anticipating remarriage should plan carefully. There are the practical questions —where you will live, how you will allocate money, how household responsibilities will be divided. And there are the emotional issues, such as how your commitment to your partner squares with your commitment to your children. Plainly, there is need for good communication with your intended about the goals of both of you. Some parents find that they can benefit from professional counseling in the weeks before the marriage.

The absent biological parent often casts a long shadow in a remarried family. In a sense, he is psychologically present in the new household, and your children will need regular contact with him, no matter how difficult that may be for you to fit in with your other scheduled activities. Stepparents, for their part, have to realize that they cannot replace a biological parent and really should not even try. If this is a disappointment to them at first, they will soon discover that they can still have a major effect on the spouse's children—as friend, mentor, role model, or all of these. It is best to let stepparenting evolve naturally rather than to try to force it.

In thinking about what name your child should use when addressing the stepparent, you may favor "Mommy" or "Daddy." By implication, however, this denies the existence of the biological parent and may well upset the child. Toddlers are often comfortable with a compromise arrangement, calling the stepparent by an alternate name such as Momma Sue, Poppa Jim, or Poppy; older children may prefer using the first name. Hold back and leave this decision to your child.

You and your new spouse will need to work out a strategy for disciplining the children. Until the family settles into a natural rapport, it is generally best for the biological parent to set and enforce the rules. This approach permits the stepparent to build ties to the children without having to be an authority figure, which, likely as not, would antagonize them. Your children must understand, however, that if you are not around and discipline is necessary, the stepparent has an obligation to provide it, and the youngster to accept it. And if a child's misbehavior is specifically directed at the new parent, the stepparent should be the one to respond to it.

In the beginning, the more realistic everyone's expectations for family life are, the better off the stepfamily will be. Harmony and trust do not happen overnight, and love between stepparent and child develops gradually. Research has shown that it takes anywhere from two to seven years for a strong bond to form. Initially, acceptance of differences is more important than love in nurturing the relationship.

The impact on your children

While your remarriage is a joyous occasion for you, your child may harbor a variety of emotions. With your wedding comes the death of the youngster's secretly held fantasy that you might reunite with your former spouse. As the child settles into new family relationships, he often experiences feelings not only of loss, but also of anger, resentment, and displacement.

He may resist the stepparent's offer of friendship even though he already knows the person well. From the outset, he needs assurances that your new family will survive even though the previous one failed. Let him know that you are making a lifetime commitment, and that even though there are bound to be problems along the way, you are determined to remain steadfast and see them through.

The older the youngster, the more difficult the adjustment is likely to be. Experts agree that children under three usually have the easiest time accepting a stepparent. But even the youngest child may go through a difficult period of adjustment. Your toddler, knowing that he has already "lost" one parent, may begin to hover near you, worrying you will leave as well. Ease the transition as much as you can by making sure that you, your child, and your spouse spend plenty of time together. If you are moving into your new partner's home, bring along as many familiar furnishings as you can. And, if possible, avoid too many changes in the child's routines.

Helping their father paint the clubhouse brings these stepsiblings together. The end result of this shared labor is a plaything that belongs equally to all.

If your youngster is a preschooler, be prepared for temper tantrums, nightmares, bedwetting, and generally regressive behavior. All of these may be signs that the youngster needs extra attention. It is also possible that your child will feel guilty about liking his new stepparent. He may regard the attachment as disloyalty to his real Daddy or Mommy. Help him to understand that he can care for a variety of people without hurting any of them.

Stepsibling relationships

Along with the new stepparent there may be one or more new siblings for your child to integrate into her life. When she suddenly finds herself having brothers and sisters where there were none before, her world can seem topsy-turvy indeed. No longer the only child, she has a new and unfamiliar place in the pecking order. To make matters worse, that troublesome concept "share" can now seem like a standing order. Children in remarried families are asked not only to share their parents, but often their rooms and their precious toys.

It should come as no surprise then that children in remarried families fight with their stepsiblings as they jockey for position. Whenever possible, avoid interfering in their spats; the children are usually quite capable of working out their differences themselves. And remember that you cannot force them to love each other any more than you can require them to like each other. Affection will probably come in time as mutual respect and the fund of shared experiences grow.

No matter how cramped your new household may be, make sure that each child has at least some special space that she can call her own. Even children who visit only on weekends need a corner, a shelf, or at the very least a drawer that they consider theirs. More important, they need time alone each day with their biological parent to share feelings, recall happy memories, and soak up love.

Before getting married, look for ways to foster togetherness among the children. In a sense, you need to court the entire family. Plan a variety of activities—shopping, picnicking, or sightseeing—that give everyone a chance to interact. Once all the children live together in the household, they are likely to adjust more easily.

One way that many remarried parents cement their new family ties is to have a baby of their own. Children under five may feel particularly jealous and threatened by the arrival of such a sibling. But in the long run, an infant biologically connected to everyone generally unifies the family. ❖

Interracial Families

Interracial couples are, for the most part, keenly aware of society's preconceptions about race. As parents, they are forced to acknowledge that racism exists and could create difficulties for their children. Moreover, they have the peculiar problem of labeling to contend with. If a father is white and his spouse black, is their child white or black? The parents may refer to a youngster as biracial, mixed race, or even a rainbow child. But others are likely to identify the child solely by her predominant physical characteristics. If the child is to learn to appreciate her relationship to two separate racial heritages, she will need special help from her parents.

Children's awareness of racial differences

Before the age of two-and-a-half or three, racial differences that are apparent to you will not be obvious to your child. At three years of age, the youngster may ask questions about skin color, hair texture, or differences in the shapes of people's eyes. Encourage her to ask questions and talk to her in a positive way about her own physical features. Since various family members do not resemble each other, you will need to discuss the differences openly and emphasize, for example, that all shades of skin are beautiful. In your discussions, avoid suggesting that certain physical characteristics are exotic, which can make her feel uncomfortable.

An awareness of race and well-defined feelings about racial differences begin to appear in the preschool years. The child's attitudes are shaped by many influences—principally by her observations of how you regard people of all races, but also by things you cannot

Good communication is all the more important when a youngster has to integrate two racial identities. He will take his cues chiefly from his parents in forming his attitudes about race.

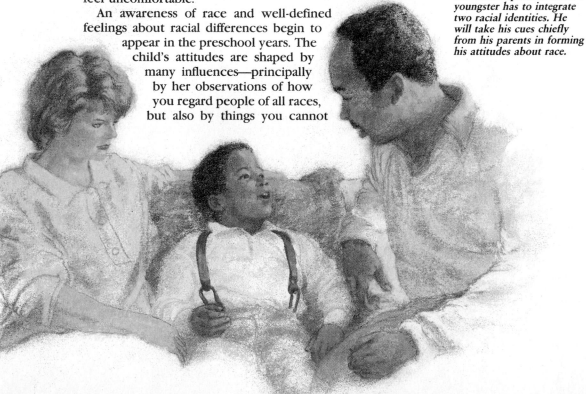

111

control, such as conversations she overhears and television programs she sees in her friends' homes. At this tender age, she realizes that others have pigeonholed her in a racial group.

Helping a child with identity issues

Your child needs pride in his racial background. It helps to live in a mixed neighborhood and send your child to an integrated day-care center or nursery school where racial differences are not a cause for concern. Most important is your own sense of racial and cultural identity and your willingness to share your feelings with him.

At times your child may be upset by the fact that he does not look like you. When this happens, bolster his self-esteem by telling him how much you admire his physical features. You might also point out some of the traits that he does share with you—that both of you are left-handed, for example, and both wrinkle your noses when you laugh. This is particularly important if you have adopted a child of another race. At the same time, help your child to understand that every person has an inner beauty that does not depend on looking like anyone else.

It can also be disturbing for a child to realize that his self-image differs from how others see him. A preschooler may squabble with another child over whether he is black or brown, or may cry when a friend says that he must speak Chinese because his eyes are slanted. Your child depends on you to sort out confusions about cultural identity.

Owning an ethnic doll gives the part-Filipino girl at left a chance to mother a baby who she feels is just like herself. Having toys that feature cultural differences helps children strengthen their identification.

Confronting prejudice

Although your child may not encounter overt prejudice until she is older, comments about race often begin during preschool years. Other children may ask innocent questions, such as "Why is she black? Is she dirty?" And adults may offer ignorant compliments such as "She's very pretty for what she is." Never let a racial slur pass without correcting it on the spot, if possible. Give straightforward answers to children's questions about such incidents and, perhaps later, explore your child's feelings concerning them. Make it clear to your child that you are proud of her and love her unequivocally. ❖

Adoptive Families

The arrival of a child is a joyous occasion and nowhere more so than in an adoptive family. After months or years of trying to become parents, you find that the wait is finally over. Yet the first weeks with the new child in your home can be a time of great stress. For one thing, you may receive very little notice before the youngster arrives. In a larger sense, as well, the experience of adopting your child will be a very different experience from giving birth. You are accepting responsibility for someone else's child, at whatever age or stage the youngster may be. The first days, weeks, and months will be a time of strangers coming together to form a family.

Many adoptive parents worry about their feelings toward the child during the initial period of adjustment, when they are struggling to cope with the many new demands of parenthood. They say they do not really feel like the mother or father: They have responsibility for the child and some attachment, but they do not yet experience any great love or even a powerful bond. This may be particularly true if the child is unresponsive, poorly behaved, or favors one new parent over the other.

As anyone who has been a part of an adoptive family will assure you, love does develop as you and the child get to know one another. Research has shown that strong bonds do form in adoptive families but that it is impossible to predict how long it will be before you feel that a youngster is truly your own. While "instant love" can happen, everyone has a personal timetable in his emotions. There is no reason to feel guilty if your feelings are lukewarm at first.

Easing children into the family

In general, the younger the child, the easier the transition from one home to another. Newborns and very young infants may show no sign of having noticed the change. Older infants and toddlers, on the other hand, are more aware of their surroundings and may have formed attachments to their previous caregivers. They will find their own ways to express their grief or disorientation at the change. The baby may turn down food, vomit formula, develop diarrhea, or suffer sleep disorders. The toddler may reject the toys you offer, refuse to smile, or even cry inconsolably. You can ease the transition by finding out what you can about his routine in the previous home and sticking to it for the first few weeks. If you can bring a favorite toy or blanket from the last home, that too will soften the change. Although your child may resist affection at first, you will want to find ways to foster togetherness through feeding, bathing, snuggling, and eye contact.

Parents who adopt preschool-age children often find that their lives together start out happy and calm, then turn stormy later on. Experts refer to the peaceful phase following the youngster's arrival as the "honeymoon" period. The child may actually be in emotional turmoil, but he is trying hard to fit into the new family. The honeymoon may last anywhere from a few days to a few weeks and is usually followed by a tumultuous period in which the child is, by turns, purposely unruly and saddeningly distant or depressed. Although you may be tempted to respond to temper tantrums by withholding outward expressions of love from your youngster, make a point of overriding your reaction and offering a hug anyway. Such moments are a real opportunity to get closer to the child.

No matter how painful it may be to see your child upset, encourage him to express his feelings. Let him know that you understand his confusion and ambivalence, that it is natural to feel that way and perfectly acceptable to let such feelings show. Be prepared for sudden swings in mood and sensitive to the fact that adopted children are all the more prone to anxieties when they are separated from you. If you leave your child in day care while you work, make a special effort to pick him up on time each day. He may worry that you are going to disappear as his previous caregivers did.

If you are adopting a child from a foreign country, the youngster has additional adjustments to make in moving from one culture to another. Even a very small child may be affected by the changes in time, diet, language, or even the ways that people handle and carry babies. Before your child arrives, learn all you can about his native culture and try not to force too many changes on him at once.

Handling adoption   Most experts agree that children should know from an early age that they are adopted and that the parents should be the ones to tell them. Some people fear that revealing this information will diminish their stature as parents. But it is important for a youngster to come to terms with this aspect of his personal history. And it will not help if he hears the news from someone else or senses that you have hidden the story.

Begin talking to your child about his adoption while he is still a toddler. Be sure to broach the subject in a warm and loving manner—perhaps while holding the child on your lap and leafing through his baby album. Tell him how happy you were when he first came into your home, and how glad you are that you adopted him. Repeat this discussion from time to time as

he grows older. The early conversations may be short and simple, but they will be good practice for the tougher questions that the child will ask later on.

Repetition of the discussion is essential. Research has shown that children younger than six or seven do not yet have the cognitive ability to understand the difference between being born into a family and being adopted. In the preschooler's mind, blood ties are irrelevant, and anyone who lives with him is part of the family. Even if he tells you the story of his own adoption, he is simply parroting information he has heard and does not really comprehend it. Thus you should not be surprised if a six-year-old, who has "known" all along that he was adopted, asks you such things as: "Did I grow inside your body?" The child's understanding will deepen with age, but you might have to cover the same ground time and time again.

For an adopted child to develop a clear grasp of his identity, he has to accept the fact that he was adopted and learn to face his feelings and fantasies about his biological parents. He will have many questions about his origins and will rely on you to answer them (*box, page 117*). As he matures, he

The first days at home for a newly adopted infant are a time for settling in. It is a good idea to temporarily restrict the flow of visitors so that the family has a chance to adjust.

will want to know more
and more details.

If your adoptive child
is of another race, you
will need to make sure
that she learns about
her ethnic heritage.
She must also be pre-
pared for the peculiar
ways that people exhibit
racial prejudices to children (*page 112*). Your child
may be particularly upset
that she does not physically
resemble you or her siblings. It
is not always true that she has
a low self-image if she tells you
that she wishes she looked like
you. She may simply be stating
her love for you. Nevertheless, as with the child of an
interracial marriage, it is
wise to encourage her to
take pride in her appearance. Comment on her physical attrac-
tiveness and point out what you have in common.

On any outing, such as this one to the zoo, adoptive parents of minority children have to be prepared for questions from strangers concerning their children. Not all of the remarks will be entirely diplomatic.

While parents tend to emphasize the special or unique
qualities of their offspring, most children prefer to be just like
everybody else. An adopted child may be embarrassed by his
special status, since it sets him off from his friends. Attending
social functions run by a support group for adoptive parents
will show him that he is "just like" a number of other children
who have shared the same experiences.

Sibling relationships

When you are planning to adopt, carefully explain the situation
to your other children. Begin your discussion with simple,
straightforward explanations of the two ways that children can
become part of a family. Give the children as many details as
you can about the new sibling. If the prospective sibling is an
infant, prepare your children much as you would if you were
expecting to give birth to a baby yourself (*page 58*). If you are
adopting an older child, help your children understand that the
adjustment process may be difficult and let them help you with
any necessary preparations. Expect your children's questions
about adoption to continue for a long time. And be sure that

they are able to explain adoption to others—their friends will probably be asking questions too.

While tight sibling bonds will eventually form, you can expect that your child will probably be jealous at first. If your youngster understands that his new brother or sister came from someplace else, he may express his resentment by suggesting that the interloper be sent back. Such rivalry is normal and should not be suppressed. But find an opportunity to take the child aside and explain that it takes time to learn to love new people. Also make it clear that the new brother or sister is going to stay.

Families with both biological and adopted children have certain special emotional concerns. If you give birth to a child after adopting one, you have to make sure that the adopted child does not feel slighted or rejected. At the same time, you do not want to suggest to any of the children that being adopted is better or more special than being born into the family. Make clear to everyone that both adopted and biological children are equally your own.

What to tell others

Prudent parents sit down before the adoption and discuss what they will tell other people about the adopted child. If you confide too many details to too many relatives, you cannot guarantee that they will not let slip information that you have not had a chance to carefully explain to your children. You will even want to consider what details the adoption announcement is going to include.

The background information that the adoption agency supplies is for your use alone. It may later be of interest to the adopted child as well. The youngster's physician needs an accurate medical history, including details about the biological parents, but your next-door neighbors do not. You will probably want to tell school personnel that your child is adopted but that is all they need to know.

However carefully you think through your explanations of these matters, you may be taken aback by some of the insensitive remarks that you hear from strangers. Adoptive parents report that common questions include: "Are you the baby-sitter?" and "What do you know about the real parents?" In responding to remarks like these, remember that they are probably prompted by a lack of understanding about adoption. It is perfectly all right to say that the question is inappropriate. But if your child is listening, it also a good idea to answer questions and thus avoid confusing the youngster. In any event you will want to make it perfectly clear that the real parent is you. ❖

Talking about Adoption

Listen carefully to your adopted child's questions and keep your answers short and simple. When she is older, you can add more details. But until she is about four, answers as simple as these are sufficient.

- Q. What does "adopted" mean?
- A. It is one way that children come into a family.
- Q. Where did I come from?
- A. You came from a special place in a woman's body.
- Q. Why did my Mommy give me away?
- A. She could not take care of a child.
- Q. Who is my real Mommy?
- A. I am. You did not come from my body, but I have taken care of you, and that is why Daddy and I are your real family.

6 Building a Happy Life Together

Who does not want a happy, stable family life? Little could be of more importance to the emotional development and well-being of a child. It provides the security in which a youngster thrives and serves as a base for learning important values that she will carry with her into adulthood.

Establishing a good family life is one of the primary responsibilities that you face as a parent. At first glance, the prospect may seem overwhelming, particularly if your own family background was less than stable. Every parent, however, can create a milieu in which the qualities and traditions that help make families strong flourish. All it takes is commitment—and time.

Time spent together is the crucial element in a happy family, and the one often hardest to contrive. But experts on the family leave no doubt that the strongest families are generally those that share hours in planned activities, such as a weekly family game night; or unplanned ones, such as a spontaneous picnic on a beautiful summer day (*opposite*).

This section of the book suggests ways you can enrich your family life. It describes the qualities that inspire cohesiveness and offers ideas on how you and your partner can help foster these by creating your own special family traditions and customs. It also discusses the importance of grandparents and other relatives, as well as that of pets. And it describes how recordkeeping can embellish a sense of heritage and unity, making the family feel itself unique.

What Makes Families Strong?

"All happy families resemble one another," wrote Russian novelist Leo Tolstoi, and in many respects he was right. Researchers who have studied strong, close-knit families have identified six qualities they share: commitment, a desire to spend time together, an ability to communicate about feelings and other important matters, an appreciation of one another, spiritual beliefs, and a capacity for coping with problems.

A strong family is not necessarily the traditional nuclear family, with both the mother and father living at home. A single parent can also create a stable, nurturing environment that provides a deep sense of belonging. And remarried families—those that include children from previous marriages—can also blend into a strong unit.

Focusing on the family

When pollsters ask people what is most important to happiness, the overwhelming majority give the same response: a good family life. Most individuals need the care, comfort, and security that a resilient, loving family provides. But a conscious effort is necessary to ensure that a family is happy. It is all too easy for overtaxed parents to find themselves giving their children only leftover time, those brief stretches when they are not at their jobs, running the house, paying bills, mowing the lawn, or doing one of the countless other tasks that can quickly consume the hours of a day.

The only solution is to decide, in advance, that the family comes first. Parents must work as a team to see that careers, hobbies, and causes do not get in the way of the family's deeper needs. Thus a mother may turn down a job promotion because it would mean more traveling—and more time away from her family. A father may drop out of his bowling league for the summer so he can spend more evenings playing ball with his five-year-old son. Such parents do not devote themselves exclusively to their children, but they clearly know where their priorities lie, and their young ones feel it, too.

The gift of time together

Happy families spend a great deal of time together—playing, going on trips, or just sitting around enjoying one another. The occasion may be as simple as an after-dinner walk to a park on a nice evening; or it may be planned, like an annual camping

A mother lovingly embraces her son, showing her appreciation for the bouquet of clover and dandelions he has just picked for her. Such open and mutual signs of affection make for strong relationships.

During a family softball game, a son learns that his parents, too, have their playful—and even silly—side, but what is more important, he is reminded that they enjoy spending time with him.

trip. Family times do not always involve relaxation or play, either. A family work project can be just as satisfying if everyone has a task and takes pride in a job well done.

Many families schedule a family night each week when the members gather to pursue a single activity. The activity does not have to be elaborate or expensive; it might be one as simple as piecing together a jigsaw puzzle, viewing slides or home movies, or making cookies. What is important is that the entire family shares the experience and the memories.

The importance of communication

Because close-knit families do many things together, the members also tend to spend a lot of time talking—and listening—to one another. In fact, they make a point of keeping in touch. A father listens attentively to his four-year-old's tale about his show-and-tell experience at a play group; a mother, sensing her son's concerns about attending kindergarten for the first time, sits down with him to chat about his feelings and to tell what her own first day was like. Frequent talking about events and emotions stimulates expression and helps fortify the members so that they are able to cope well when problems arise. Many families schedule regular weekly or monthly conferences to discuss important matters.

Breaking bread

As good a place as any for the family to converse and share the day's events is at the table. Make it a point to have at least one meal each day together. Experts say that there is virtually no family event that has more symbolic and practical value in making people feel relaxed and content than sharing a meal. Reduce other potential distractions to a minimum and encourage active participation in the conversation by all. When your children are very young, you may find their mealtime performance sometimes disruptive, but eating with you, listening to you and your mate talk about what is on your minds, having a chance to join in are all important ways for them to learn about their parents' values and concerns and enhance their growing sense of self-esteem.

Mutual appreciation

Affirming and supporting one another is fundamental to family stability and a good life together. Everyone should be encouraged to show affection, whether it be through hugs, kisses, and smiles, or verbally, with words of praise. Let phrases such as "Thank you," "I'll help you," "Let's do it together," "You did a great job" and—most important—"I love you" be common currency in your family. Such expressions build a young child's self-esteem and help create a positive atmosphere in the home.

Shared beliefs

Fundamental to family strength is having a spiritual or moral faith that helps the members transcend themselves and feel part of something bigger, and of greater purpose. This belief can express itself through membership in a church, synagogue, or temple, and participation in all the attendant rituals and holidays. It can also be transmitted to children through the family's active participation in a secular cause that aids other people or expresses concern for the community at large, whether it be sponsoring foster children, helping the elderly, or participating actively in politics.

Tackling problems head on

Family strength is no absolute insurance against trouble. Sickness, money problems, death, or other stressful events befall even the most insulated of families. But research has shown that resilient families are better equipped to cope than ones with rigid attitudes. For one thing, a strong family already has in place the routines, emotional dynamics, and faith or belief that enable it to mobilize itself in a crisis. If a parent loses a job, for example, the family might call a meeting to decide ways for everyone to help cut expenses. If a loved one becomes seriously ill, the family knows that it can reach out for help. Members of strong families still get angry and depressed when trouble strikes, but they have learned how to confront rather than deny reality and to reach out instead of withdrawing. And in accepting their problems, they have learned also how to keep them in perspective, knowing that the family will hold together whatever the hurdles are that face them. ❖

The significance of being christened is lost on the baby below, but as part of a family that has spiritual roots he will develop a sense of belonging.

Grandparents' Sympathetic Magic

The bond between grandparent and grandchild could not be a more special one; in many families, it is second only to the relationship between parent and child in its emotional influence. To a youngster, a grandmother or grandfather is a kind of storyteller, sympathizer, and sage all rolled into one. Cast in such a role, grandparents often discover to their surprise that they are actually better as grandparents than they ever were as parents. Without the responsibilities and anxieties of raising children and earning a living simultaneously, they are truly free for the first time to enjoy children as children.

A living link Because people are enjoying longer and healthier lives than they did in past generations, children now have an excellent chance of developing long-lasting relationships with their grandparents, which contributes importantly to the child's growing sense of the family. Children delight in hearing their grandparents tell stories of what their parents were like when they were little, as well as hearing about events in the family's history, such as how an ancestor came to the United States from another country or how Uncle Fred saved a neighbor from a burning house when he was fourteen.

Grandparents can play a variety of other important roles in the life of a child. They can serve as a kind of confidante to her, listening to her hurts, cares, and worries and offering their own special kind of solace. They can become teachers and mentors as well, inspiring an interest in activities and hobbies, from baking bread to making airplane models and collecting stamps.

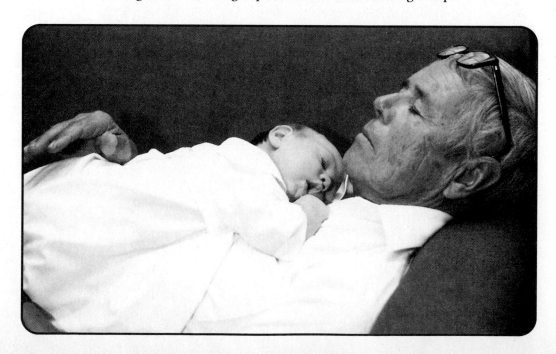

Grandparents also offer children a unique look at life and aging. Studies show that youngsters who are close to their grandparents have a better understanding of what growing old means and thus develop a perspective on the life cycle many other children lack.

Despite their differences in age, this youngster and her grandmother enjoy each other's company. In time, Grandma's stories and family legends will give the child a deeper appreciation of her family heritage.

Cultivating the bond

You can do much to foster a close relationship between your child and her grandparents.

If your parents or those of your spouse live nearby, make a point of the family getting together with them regularly. As long as they are up to it and enjoy it, encourage them to spend time alone with your child as well.

If your child's grandparents live too far away for frequent get-togethers, help nurture the grandchild-grandparent relationship with regular long-distance phone calls. Between telephone visits, encourage your child to keep a list of things she wants to tell her grandparents so she will be ready and eager to talk when the call is made. Also ask the grandparents to send letters, cards, and photographs of themselves to your child. To ensure that your youngster is on the giving as well as the receiving end of her relationship with them, have her respond to mail from the grandparents with some of her own drawings and homemade cards. Or have her send a spoken letter in the form of an audiotape or a videotape. In return, the grandparents might tape stories or recollections for the child to listen to at bedtime.

Keeping the peace

From time to time, frictions between parents and grandparents arise over differences in child-rearing techniques. Some grandparents, for example, constantly offer unwanted advice on how the children should be raised. They may complain that the parents are not feeding the grandchild right, or not disciplining him enough, or not dressing him warmly enough. If this is a problem in your family, tell the grandparent politely but firmly that although you welcome her concern, you have final responsibility for your child and will decide how best to raise him. Repeat the speech each time the grandparent interferes; eventually, the message will take hold. Some parents find it helpful to busy themselves elsewhere when their parents and children get together; that way, direct conflicts over how a child is being raised are kept to a minimum.

Some grandparents have unrealistic expectations of children, particularly of young ones. They may no longer remember how stubborn or rambunctious a toddler can be, or how a preschooler loves to explore and climb. In order to help keep visits with these grandparents pleasant and calm, prepare your youngster ahead of time, especially if you will be at the grandparents' home. Explain the fundamental rules of being a good guest to your child, such as no climbing on the furniture or no eating in the living room. Also, be sure to pack a few of your youngster's favorite toys or books to keep him busy; or suggest to your mother and father that they keep an activity box filled with toys and games that your child can play with during visits.

Spoiling Many grandparents feel that it is their right to spoil their grandchildren. They get great enjoyment out of indulging them, whether it be with expensive gifts, exotic trips, or sugary foods. Although parents often worry that such indulgences will teach their children to value the grandparents more for what they can give them than for who they are, most child-development experts disagree. Children do need to have an occasional break from the rules and restrictions that are laid down by their parents. Be sure to talk with the grandparents, however, if they are indulging your child in a way that conflicts strongly with your beliefs — for example, if they allow nonstop television watching when you set limits on daily viewing, or if they are giving your child war toys when you disapprove. ∴

On a walk, a toddler and her great-grandfather enjoy a cozy companionship. It is a special bond, one that she will remember for years to come.

Suitable Pets for Children under Six

A pet can be a genuine member of the family, and one that holds a unique place in a child's heart. Like parents and grandparents, a dog or a cat can give its affection to a child unstintingly. With parental guidance, a pet will also instill a sense of responsibility in a child and help him develop nurturing attitudes.

Useful and delightful though a pet may be, it should not be brought into the home without forethought. In choosing a pet, take into account its exercise and space requirements, whether it needs training or grooming, and just how much companionship it can be expected to provide. An apartment-dwelling family may find the exercising of a dog too much to handle and prefer a cat. A family with members who suffer from allergies may have to forgo a furry animal for a parakeet or fish.

Always keep your child's age in mind. Most preschoolers are not ready to take full responsibility for the pet, and the greater share of caring for it will fall to you. Certainly no child under six should be left unsupervised with a dog or cat; even the most lovable creature can behave in ways that might frighten or endanger a youngster, especially when provoked.

If you decide on a dog or cat, select a breed known to be gentle with children, such as a Labrador retriever or a Burmese cat. Or try to find out something about the temperament of the animal's parents, which may well be reflected in the offspring. When dogs and cats are neutered, they are generally more placid household pets.

Under no circumstances should you take wild animals as pets, even those bred in captivity; they seldom make good family companions and may turn savage or introduce disease. You can, however, encourage your child to "adopt" a wild animal, either by setting up bird or other animal feeders in your backyard or by making frequent visits to your local zoo or nature center to watch a favorite animal eating and playing.

The list of animals on these two pages should assist you in choosing an appropriate pet for your youngster.

Recommended Breeds

Dogs
- medium-size breeds: spaniels and beagles
- larger breeds: retrievers, collies, setters, and boxers
- very small breeds: avoid these; they tend to be excitable

Cats
- domestic shorthairs, Burmese, Abyssinian
- long-hair breeds: avoid these; children may pull hair

Fish
- goldfish; guppies or other tropical fish

Rodents
- gerbils and guinea pigs
- hamsters: not as highly recommended; become active mainly at night and can inflict a painful bite

Birds
- parakeets, canaries, and cockatiels

Costs

- mixed-breed dogs often free or cost less than $20; purebred pups, $75 to $600
- annual expenses for licensing, food, vaccinations, and other veterinary services between $150 and $700
- veterinarian's fee for neutering male dogs $50; spaying females, $60 to $150; check animal shelters for special rates

- mixed-breed cats often free or cost less than $10; purebred kittens $125 to $300
- annual expenses for food, vaccinations, and other veterinary services between $150 and $210
- fee for neutering male cats about $30; spaying females, $60; check animal shelters for special rates

- small goldfish and guppies often priced under $1; some larger fish and exotic tropical breeds cost $40 or more
- tanks and aquarium equipment start at about $30
- annual cost for food and plants: $15 to $30

- purchase price: $2 to $25
- cage and equipment: $10 to $40
- annual expenses for food, bedding, and veterinary services: between $30 and $40

- sell for $15 to $80
- cage and extra equipment cost between $30 and $75
- annual expenses for food and veterinary services between $40 and $50

Space and Exercise Requirements	Temperament and Care	Life Span
• medium-size dogs need outside doghouse or average-size room for sleeping, as well as space to run outside • some large breeds sedentary; most need wide-open spaces for exercise • indoor dogs must be walked at least three times a day to prevent kidney problems	• can be very affectionate and devoted; depends in part upon breeding • male dogs usually more aggressive; more likely to wander from home, especially if unneutered • large dogs often more patient with children • best to get a puppy that grows up with family or an adult dog used to being around children • dogs need significant companionship, praise, and training • regular bathing, brushing, and flea treatment required	• medium breeds: 10-14 years • large breeds: 7-9 years
• a permanent, sanitary, convenient location needed for a litter box; clean daily and change weekly • all cats need scratching post or they may damage furniture with their claws; if kept indoors exclusively, consider declawing	• temperaments range from very aloof to extremely affectionate; friendlier when raised from kittens in family • most will scratch if abused by a child • easily trained to use a litter box, but usually do not respond to obedience training • some grooming needed to minimize formation of hair balls • both males and females make better pets if neutered	• 10-17 years • outdoor cats more prone to disease and injury; shorter life span
• a 5½-gallon tank suitable for fewer than 6 goldfish or 11 guppies • need plants, gravel, and fish net • tropical fish require water between 75° and 80° F; heating unit may be necessary • all tanks should have filters and aerators; frequent water changes increase chances of harming fish	• although generally skittish, fish anticipate feedings; may learn to take food from child's fingers • filters for tanks should be cleaned once every one to three weeks • toddler needs supervision around fish tank; danger of pulling tank down or dumping something in tank	• very prone to disease and mishandling; maximum of 1-3 years
• guinea pig needs 10-gallon fish tank or 8-inch-deep drawer with wire-mesh top; a 5- to 10-gallon aquarium will house two gerbils • pine shavings for bedding • other necessary equipment includes a hanging water bottle, food containers, chew sticks, and toys such as exercise wheels • position cage away from drafts	• gerbils' tail skin slips off if not handled properly • guinea pigs tame when treated affectionately; do not bite; nails may need to be trimmed; will coo when scratched behind the ears; will accept treats • larger guinea pigs can be let out of cage in a secure area with adult supervision • clean cages twice weekly • some long-haired guinea pigs need grooming • guinea pigs require vitamin C supplement; prone to colds and suffer in temperature extremes • gerbils produce little waste; guinea pigs messier • rodents breed often; if purchasing a pair, buy same sex	• gerbils: 2-3 years • guinea pigs: 2-4 years
• standard wire cage with dowel perches and food and water dishes that do not touch floor; must be large enough for bird to fly (check pet store for size) • position away from drafts • mirrors, toys, or swings for stimulation • can be messy, scattering seeds and feathers	• a canary mostly for watching; does not tame easily • parakeets and cockatiels may mimic whistles or other sounds; may be trained to perch on a finger • clean cage bottom daily; clean cage itself once a month • need diet supplements added to grain; check with pet store • need cuttlebone to peck on to wear down beak • easily crushed by children; will nip if startled or provoked	• 5-10 years

The Richness of a Shared Heritage

Whether they be simple peekaboo games before bedtime or annual family reunions at Granny's, traditions are at the core of a family's identity. Traditions strengthen the links among family members, building a bank of common memories, and provide a structure to family life that everyone, especially the young, can understand. Children take pleasure not only in knowing that they belong to a distinctive family, but that the family has its own way of doing things. Once a tradition takes hold, a child will often brook no deviation from it.

Establishing traditions

Many traditions arise spontaneously. A family, for example, takes a drive through some nearby mountains one autumn to view the changing colors of the trees. They decide to repeat the trip the next year, and a custom comes to be.

Other traditions are started by design, as when a family celebrates Thanksgiving in a distinctive way. Perhaps they set the table with special decorations, bring out Grandmother's fine china, say grace while linking hands, or take a formal Thanksgiving Day photo with everyone standing behind the turkey as Dad carves the first slice.

When establishing traditions for your family, begin by examining your own past. If you have warm memories of making applesauce every fall with your great-grandmother, why not renew the tradition now with your son or daughter? If you had a Sunday evening sing-along with your parents when you were little, why not revive that custom with your own family? Think of the other events that you enjoyed as a child; chances are your youngster will like them too.

Keeping the Japanese tradition of Boys' Day, a mother helps her son into a kimono like ones worn by his ancestors. Preserving the customs of the homeland can broaden a child's sense of the world—and who he is within it.

When traditions clash

With marriage, two sets of family traditions come together. Sometimes these blend easily and seamlessly, but other times it takes sensitive negotiations to satisfy all. In families that celebrate Christmas, for example, presents may be opened on Christmas Eve by candlelight or on Christmas morning before breakfast. Couples who differ on this may have to compromise, perhaps by stretching the gift opening over both days.

Sunday morning pancake breakfast, served up by Dad, is a small but important ritual in this family. To make the occasion even more special, the meal is always eaten in the dining room.

Discuss with your spouse the traditions that are most important to you and work out solutions everyone can live with.

In remarried families where stepparents and stepchildren have strong feelings about what is traditional, family customs can be even stickier. A way to gain a consensus is to add new traditions around events having no particular significance—a special dinner on Valentine's Day, for example, or a monthly Pizza Night. Save some old rituals, though, and bring the rest of the family into them, for they can help each child's transition into the blended family.

Everyday rituals Routine offers opportunities for sustaining daily rituals. Children love repetitive activities, largely because these instill a feeling of security. Sometimes a family ritual seems so commonplace that you might not think of it as such—the evening walk with the dog, for example, or the family game after dinner, or shopping with Dad on Saturday morning. These are just the kinds of rituals that your child anticipates with pleasure.

The nightly bedtime ritual is by far the most ordinary and at the same time most important of these. Try to establish a

Parent to Parent

The Stuff of Memories

❝Each summer, when strawberry season arrives, our whole family goes berry picking. The kids love it. We get up early on a Saturday morning and drive to a farm just outside the city where you can pick your own berries for a really low price. Then we bring the berries home and spend the rest of the day making jam. Everyone pitches in; last year our four-year-old daughter, Amy, helped decorate the labels for the jars. We usually make enough jam to last us all year; we also give some to friends when we go visiting.❞

❝Before I drive Dylan to his day care in the morning, I always sit down with him and read him a story. We started this ritual a year ago when I decided I wanted our mornings together to feel less rushed. Now we both look forward to the readings—they help set a quiet, relaxed tone for the day.❞

❝Sunday night is what we call 'family game night' at our house. The children have an early bath, then we all gather in the living room to play a game together. The kids take turns choosing the game. Our daughter, who is six-and-a-half, likes to play board games the best; but our son, who's four, prefers more physical games, like animal charades. After the game is over, my husband or I will read a story aloud to the kids, and then it's off to bed for them—and a nice quiet evening for us.❞

❝Our family has a silver celebration cup, and it's something that we bring out only on special occasions—birthdays, Christmas, Easter, and other eventful days. One was Erin's first day at kindergarten. We fill the cup with a nonalcoholic champagne and then, after one of us makes an impromptu toast, we pass it around the table. Everyone takes a sip. It's a way of marking important moments in our lives.❞

❝After our first son was born, my husband and I decided we would rather ring in the New Year with our family than spend it with strangers at some large, expensive celebration. When Joey was very small we did our celebrating very quietly, but now that Michael has come and we have two little boys, we always make a special night of New Year's Eve. We bundle ourselves up in warm clothes and go outside just before midnight to wish on a star and listen to all the car horns honking. Then we go back inside and treat ourselves to hot chocolate and cookies. The warmth of that evening stays with us throughout the new year.❞

pattern that is consistently warm and comforting. You might include reading a story or telling one of your own, talking over the day's events, or playing a favorite tape or record. Young children also enjoy hearing the same parting phrase from their parents each night, whether it be an affectionate "Sweet dreams" or a smile-evoking "Good night, sleep tight, don't let the bedbugs bite." And they may have very precise notions of how they want you to kiss them—once, twice, three times, from left to right or right to left.

Treasured holidays Whether it be sharing a Seder dinner, decorating a tree on Christmas Eve, or dyeing Easter eggs, holiday traditions allow families to reaffirm their shared beliefs and values. Children especially enjoy holiday celebrations. They find happiness in knowing that there are special times for special happenings, and such occasions become important markers in their lives. "That was the Christmas I got my bike," or "That was the Fourth of July when I learned how to swim in Grandpa's pond."

Although it can seem at times that children care only about treats, presents, and staying up late on holidays, studies have shown that they value the memories that come afterward as much as they do the excitement of treats. Thus it is important that parents not get so caught up in preparations for these good times that they end up too harried and hurried to give their children personal attention and make them onlookers instead of participants. If your little one is too small to cut out the eyes, nose and mouth of the Halloween pumpkin, do not insist on preparing the jack-o'-lantern all by yourself; have her scoop out the seeds and tell you the kind of face she would like. When the project is done, invite everyone to sit down to a seasonal apple cider and pumpkin pie. While your youngster is still too little to go trick-or-treating, you can have some fun at home putting on silly makeup and hats to greet the neighborhood children who come to your door. Top off the Halloween evening with the reading of a not-too-scary story.

You can make a holiday more meaningful by emphasizing the values that underlie the occasion rather than its decorations. For Valentine's Day, for example, emphasize the message of love by having an after-dinner ceremony in which members of the family tell one another something special about each other that they love. At Christmas or Hanukkah, stress the idea of giving by having your child pick out a new toy that is to be donated to a charity, such as the children's ward of a local hospital. Be sure to explain to your youngster the symbolic meaning of each holiday activity, such as how the lighting of the Hanukkah candles represents the miracle of deliverance, and how the decorated Easter egg represents rebirth.

A young boy carefully decorates a row of eggs, an activity that is part of his family's Easter tradition. Later his parents will hide them around the house and the artist will gleefully assume the role of hunter.

Rites of passage Every family has its own rites of passage—birthdays, anniversaries, baptisms, bar mitzvahs, and so on—that can be celebrated in unique and meaningful ways. Children enjoy the fuss and attention that accompanies a birthday, whether it is theirs or someone else's. Your family can establish its own birthday rituals to help make these days memorable. Serve the birthday child her dinner on a special plate that is used only on such occasions, or decorate her room with balloons and streamers during the night so that she wakes up to a colorful reminder of the important day. One very special way of commemorating a birthday is to write a letter to your child, telling her how much you love her and describing some of her accomplishments during the year. Read the letter aloud at the table and then put it away for safekeeping in her treasure box (*page 136*). Make parents' birthdays an occasion, too, because your children will find it great fun to make a fuss over you.

Rejoicing with the seasons

Seasons offer you an opportunity to create your own special family traditions. In the autumn, for example, you might plan a leaf-raking party or a family hayride at a nearby farm; in winter, ice-skating at a lake or at a rink in a city park; in spring, a planting-of-the-garden celebration or a trip to the botanical garden; and in summer, an overnight camping trip or a neighborhood watermelon party. Some families commemorate Midsummer Night (June 21, the longest day of the year) by eating dinner outdoors and watching the sun set, or the winter solstice (December 21, the shortest day of the year) with a special candlelight dinner. Adopting such celebrations is a good way to establish new rituals within a remarried family.

Spotlighting your family's heritage

Knowledge of your ancestors and their achievements can engender pride in the family's roots. Introduce your child to his heritage while he is still a baby by playing recorded music of the country or countries involved. When you read to him, make it a point to include the folktales, legends, and poems of the culture; you should be able to find such stories at your local library or bookstore.

As your child grows, take him to pertinent cultural exhibits at local museums, or to ethnic parades and festivals sponsored by civic or other organizations in your community. Serve festive meals from time to time that incorporate some of the dishes of the old country. You may also wish to set up a family heritage display, where photographs of relatives living and dead are prominently displayed, along with mementos of the

past. Keeping a scrapbook on your family's history, replete with photographs, ancient documents, letters, postcards, and even recent newspaper and magazine articles that describe what life is like in the old country today is a good idea.

Family reunions

There can be no warmer way to celebrate a family's diverse heritage than at a reunion, to which relatives come from far-flung places. It says to a child that even the extended family cares enough to take the time to get together.

Reunions work best when there are some—but not too many—organized activities. If the reunion is spread over several days, plan a different major event for each day—perhaps a picnic on the first one, a visit to some site of special significance to the family on the next, and a talent night and songfest on the final evening. The events should involve all members of the family. To ensure that the spirit lives on, record on tape some of the favorite songs and stories of the older members of the family. These tapes can be enjoyed by your child for years to come.

Taking family vacations

Annual vacations are a wonderful way for families to build lasting memories and traditions. Even the planning will foster family togetherness, particularly if all members, including the children, are included in the preparations. A four-year-old, for example, can pack her own small suitcase of favorite toys, and a six-year-old, with a little help, can mark out the proposed route on her own map, keeping the map with her on the journey to check your progress. Most children like going back to last year's spot—returning to the same lake cabin, beach house, or ski resort—but new destinations can also be exciting. Ready your child for a long trip by talking with her about where you are going and what you will be doing when you get there. Show her pictures of your destination; but also reassure her clearly that the family will come back home at the end of a fixed time.

Tips to the wise   Traveling with children understandably requires forethought. Pack only what is absolutely needed. Check ahead to see whether you can rent such baby equipment as a crib, stroller, and high chair at the final destination. (Many hotels and motels provide them free of charge.) If you arc traveling by plane with a child who has not yet been toilet-trained, take along just enough food, formula, and diapers for the duration of the flight plus twenty-four hours; additional supplies can be bought once you arrive. You can take more supplies on a car journey, but again, be careful not to overpack; you will almost always be able to buy more when needed. Include some snacks; children always get hungry in cars.

On a vacation away from the routines and distractions of home, this family wandering the seashore can renew itself and create memories that will sustain it through the winter.

To keep toddlers and pre-schoolers from becoming bored during long hours on the road or in an airplane, pack a surprise bag or box filled with new and unfamiliar toys and with such play materials as crayons and coloring paper, a small blackboard with eraser and colored chalk, punch-out sticker books, and perhaps a collection of plastic farm animals or a picture-card game. If you are planning on traveling by car, bring along a portable tape player and several new children's storybook- and song tapes. Or, better yet, make up your own songs and stories as you travel—they too will come to be part of your family's traditions. •:•

Preserving the Past
for the Future

You can contribute to family unity and pride by becoming the family archivist. Children delight in poring over old and new photographs of themselves, seeing pictures of other family members when they too were young, and reliving remembered events from their own past. One special way of emphasizing family ties and enjoying many warm moments of sharing is to put together an informal family history. This can include anything you want of practical or sentimental value—snapshots, medical records, keepsakes, tape recordings.

Begin, perhaps, with a visual record. Having a family repository of pictures, slides, home movies, and videotapes guarantees that many of childhood's fleeting moments will be preserved. One especially effective way to track a child's growth is to collect a series of "time-lapse" photos over the years: Every few months, take a photograph of your youngster against the same background and from the same distance. If you like, mount the images on a wall or put them in a special album. Be sure to date each of the pictures; you may not remember a year later precisely when they were taken. And for other photos include the location and a brief description of the occasion or activity, as well as the date; your child will enjoy having this information when he is older.

Medical records are, of course, essential to charting your youngster's growth and development; but preserved as part of your family archive, they can offer the youngster facts about himself that promote his sense of individuality. They will show him, too, that he is important in your eyes and in the doctor's. Log data on prenatal health, the type of delivery, and birth statistics, such as weight, length, and heart rate. Note the child's blood type, any allergies, special medications, illnesses, and injuries, and of course, the dates of his immunizations and of the onset of childhood diseases. From a practical standpoint such data can be invaluable later in providing diagnostic insights into health problems. To ensure safekeeping, medical records should be kept separately from items included in a keepsake box.

Equally fascinating to your child can be a journal of his behavior, in which you tell when he sat up for the first time, took his first step, talked, walked, and so on. You might also describe whether he was an active or quiet baby, a hearty or fussy eater, a sound or restless sleeper. You can write down his early dreams, as well as some of the things he said that were funny or bright. Or—if you have the chance—you can record them on tape and play them later to the delight of all. ❖

Highlighting Family History

A homemade keepsake box, decorated with birth announcement and congratulatory cards, can offer a child years of pleasure as she examines the relics of her babyhood. Among the items that might fit into this shoebox are a silver cup, a rattle, a hairbrush, a favorite soft toy, a hospital bracelet, a lock of hair, a pair of booties, and a cassette tape of baby's early vocalizations.

A large map of the United States mounted on a cork-backed bulletin board in a room that everyone uses can mark places special to a family. Here, pennants attached to colored toothpicks show where various relatives were born and live, where the family has vacationed, even where Daddy has gone this week on a business trip. In addition to being a good geography lesson, such a map helps a child develop a perception of his extended family.

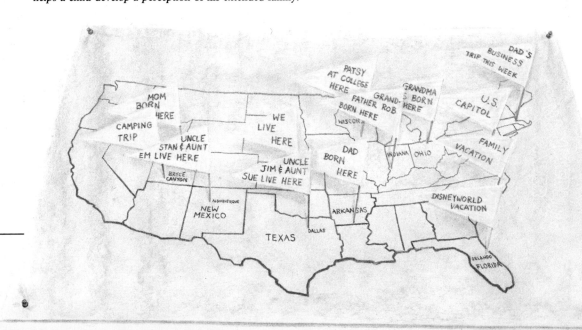

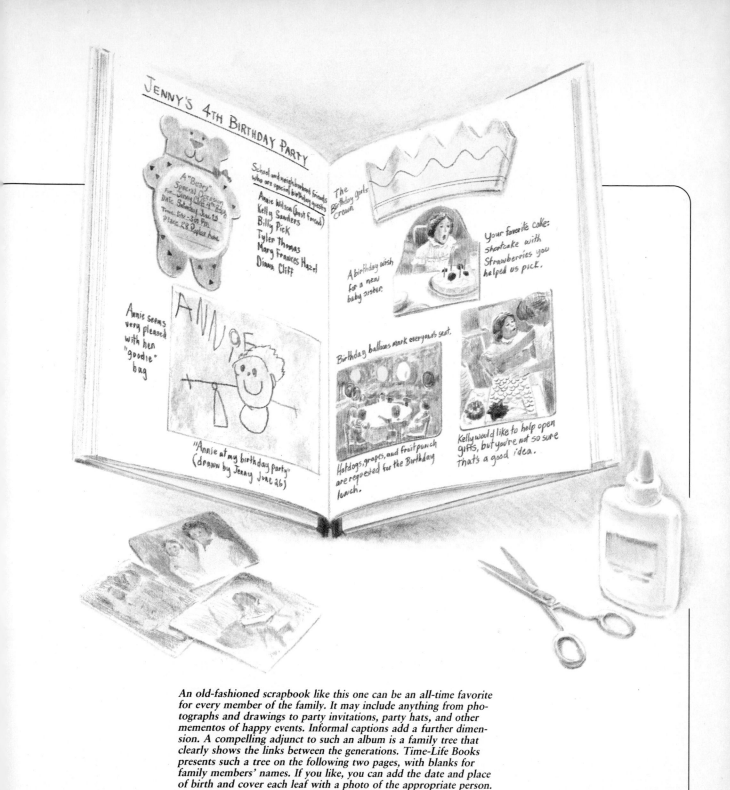

An old-fashioned scrapbook like this one can be an all-time favorite for every member of the family. It may include anything from photographs and drawings to party invitations, party hats, and other mementos of happy events. Informal captions add a further dimension. A compelling adjunct to such an album is a family tree that clearly shows the links between the generations. Time-Life Books presents such a tree on the following two pages, with blanks for family members' names. If you like, you can add the date and place of birth and cover each leaf with a photo of the appropriate person.

Great-grandmother

Grandmother

Great-grandfather

Great-grandfather

Grandfather

Great-grandmother

Mother

Maternal

The

Family Tree

Child